CIA Special Weapons & Equipment

Spy Devices of the Cold War

H. Keith Melton

Foreword by the Hon. Richard Helms, former Director of Central Intelligence

Sterling Publishing Co., Inc.   New York

Dedication

To the officers and technicians of the CIA's Technical Services Staff and the achievements for which the cloak of secrecy has prevented their personal recognition.

Acknowledgments

For their gracious assistance in the preparation of this volume:

The Hon. Richard Helms, Linda McCarthy, Exhibits Coordinator for the Central Intelligence Agency, John Minnery, Hayden B. Peake, Elizabeth Bancroft, Dan Mulvenna, Sam Halpern, MW, David Kahn, Gary Cain, Pierre Lorain, Dudley Emer, A. Ross, Jim Phillips, Maj. John Brown, Dr. Thomas Planchard, Jerry Coates, and Glynis Johnston.

With appreciation for the use of the following photographs and material: John Minnery, pages 12, 14, 17, 19, 20, 23, 98, 99, 114; Dr. Walter L. Pforzheimer, pages 8, 10; Jim Phillips, page 103; CIA, page 122.

Artwork necessary for this volume has been prepared by John Miguez of Impact Advertising.

With Special Recognition

Dr. Walter L. Pforzheimer, the CIA's first Legislative Counsel, Dean of Intelligence Bibliophiles, and curator of the extraordinary Pforzheimer Collection.

10 9 8 7 6 5 4 3 2 1

First paperback edition published in 1994 by
Sterling Publishing Company, Inc.
387 Park Avenue South, New York, N.Y. 10016
© 1993 by H. Keith Melton
Distributed in Canada by Sterling Publishing
% Canadian Manda Group, P.O. Box 920, Station U
Toronto, Ontario, Canada M8Z 5P9
Distributed in Great Britain and Europe by Cassell PLC
Villiers House, 41/47 Strand, London WC2N 5JE, England
Distributed in Australia by Capricorn Link (Australia) Pty Ltd.
P.O. Box 6651, Baulkham Hills, Business Centre, NSW 2153
Manufactured in the United States of America
All rights reserved

Sterling ISBN 0-8069-8732-4 Trade
0-8069-8733-2 Paper

Library of Congress Cataloging-in-Publication Data

Melton, H. Keith (Harold Keith), 1944–
    CIA special weapons & equipment : spy devices of the Cold War /
H. Keith Melton ; foreword by Richard Helms.
        p.   cm.
    Includes bibliographical references and index.
    ISBN 0-8069-8732-4
    1. Military intelligence—United States—Equipment and supplies—
Handbooks, manuals, etc.   2. Sabotage—United States—Equipment and
supplies—Handbooks, manuals, etc.   3. Espionage—United States—
Equipment and supplies—Handbooks, manuals, etc.   I. Title.
II. Title: CIA special weapons and equipment.
UB271.U5M43   1993
355.3'432'028—dc20   92-35849
                                                                          CIP
Edited by Rodman van Oss Neumann

Contents

Foreword

The tools of espionage have changed greatly from the "suitcase radio" days of secret operations in OSS during World War II. In the post-war era, for example, the much improved smaller and faster versions of communications gear, surveillance devices, cameras, and secret writing techniques were made possible by the transistor and other new inventions. The CIA was quick to adapt the new technology for its purposes, a process which has continued into the era of the microchip and satellite communications. This book ends in 1970, so that the author could avoid compromising any materials in current use.

As technology gradually made the old tools obsolete, they were put aside and often forgotten. We are indebted to H. Keith Melton as a private citizen for spending the time to study and to acquire these items of clandestine tradecraft, which are now housed in his unequalled private collection. Thanks to his efforts, these often unique and always fascinating devices, once so sensitive and highly classified, are now explained and illustrated in this splendid book.

The selection of the tradecraft devices and equipment from Melton's collection illustrated in this volume include, for example, the "Button Hole" Robot camera, the wristwatch camera, a cigarette pack camera, an inflatable (and flyable) rubber aeroplane, and a miniature one-man submarine. The items selected also are frequently accompanied by unique illustrations taken from their original instruction manuals. Professionals are often having to be advised to try reading the instructions before attempting to use their equipment!

This book is the product of 17 years of persistent effort by Keith Melton to prevent the extinction of the devices on which so many intelligence officers came to depend. For this he deserves great credit from the public, and especially from many of us who once used this equipment.

Richard Helms
Former Director of Central Intelligence

Former Director Helms (on right) is seen in this 1991 photograph reviewing items found in the former headquarters of the East German Secret Police (Stazi) with the author (on left).

The Hon. Richard McGarrah Helms, Director of Central Intelligence from 30 June 1966 to 2 February 1973.

Introduction

In 1952 a tiny "bugging" device was found within the wooden "Great Seal" that hung above the ambassador's desk in Moscow. The thought of the Soviets eavesdropping on the US Ambassador was serious, but an examination of the device was even more alarming. CIA Technical Services Staff (TSS) experts were studying the first "passive cavity transmitter" to be discovered by Western intelligence services. It was about as large around as a quarter, and eleven-sixteenths of an inch deep; attached to it was a thin antenna rod nine inches long. It used no batteries, no wires, no switches, and elevated the science of audio monitoring to a level previously thought to be impossible. This sophisticated and complex technology overshadowed CIA capabilities in audio monitoring that relied upon commercial law enforcement equipment and antiquated World War II telephone company listening devices.

For the United States to prevail in a "cold war" with the Soviets, improvements in clandestine technology would have to be forthcoming. US achievements in science and technology would have to be reflected somehow in the world of CIA tradecraft.

In this book I hope to give the reader an idea of the specialized tools and equipment that subsequently became available to the US intelligence community during the height of the Cold War (circa 1962). Though many of the devices shown herein were developed exclusively for the CIA, some devices, such as the Minox camera and Minifon recorder, were of civilian origin. This equipment was used not only by the CIA, but also by other Western intelligence agencies around the world. Other equipment such as the Document Copying Attaché Case was developed by Military Intelligence, but used by the CIA and others. In general then, espionage equipment, regardless of which intelligence agency created it, was often made available to "friendly" services.

This is not a study based on "official" sources; all the files necessary for such an undertaking have not been released. Nevertheless, it is the result of a twenty-year investigation that has taken me to libraries, museums, archives, bookstores, back rooms, and private collections in the US, Canada, and Europe. Estimates of the dates when specific pieces of equipment were used have been made based on my best information. In some cases they can only be deduced from the level of technology involved.

The Central Intelligence Agency, for obvious reasons, does not label or imprint its tradecraft equipment with its name, or the initials "CIA." Still there remain many practical clues that may be used by historians to establish reasonable provenance of the intelligence equipment pictured herein:

• Equipment developed for the Office of Strategic Services (OSS) during World War II served as the technical foundation of the CIA in 1947. Our extensive knowledge of OSS R&D (Research and Development) gives us a window into the technical beginnings of its successor, the CIA. The alphabetical system used to identify some OSS equipment was adopted and only modified slightly for use by the CIA. (Example: The OSS's first clandestine radio was the SSTR-1; it stood for **S**pecial **S**ervices **T**ransmitter **R**eceiver-**1**. Individual components of the SSTR-1 were the SSR-1 (Special Services Receiver-1), SST-1 (Special Services Transmitter-1), and SSP-1 (Special Services Power Supply-1).

• Memoirs written by former CIA veterans occasionally mention specific items of equipment. Harry Rositzke's reference to the "big RS-1 transceiver" (*CIA's Secret Operations*, Reader's Digest Press, New York, 1977, page 31) and Philip Agee's reference to the "SRR-4" surveillance radio (*CIA Diary: Inside the Company*, Stonehill Publishing, New York, 1975, page 95) not only document use of the specific device, but more importantly provide clues to other related pieces of equipment using similar designations. Each one of the examples above did lead to further identifications; e.g., the RS-6 (Radio Station-6); RR/D-11 (Radio Receiver/D-11); SSR-5 (Special Surveillance Receiver-5).

- Manuals and instruction sheets accompanying some pieces of equipment provide clues to their origin. Though the manuals invariably carry no security classification or name of issuing agency, with careful analysis they can sometimes be recognized by the consistency in their layout, design, artwork, and type fonts.

- The Freedom of Information Act, in the mid-1970s, spawned the release and publication of a number of CIA manuals:

  1) *CIA Flaps and Seals Manual*, edited by John M. Harrison, 1975; shown within is the Model-1 Hotplate on page 16, and the Flaps and Seals (envelope opening) tools, page 6. Information contained in the book led to the subsequent identification of the Flaps and Seals Kit.
  2) *CIA Explosives Supply Catalog*, no publisher or publication date; the manual is internally dated 1 July 1966. Shown within are a wide variety of explosive, incendiary, and sabotage devices including Federal Stock Numbers (FSN) for ordering.
  3) *CIA Special Weapon Supply Catalog*, no publisher or publication date; shown within are a wide variety of explosive, incendiary, and sabotage devices including FSNs for ordering. In addition, page 47 provides details on the 9-mm "Deer Gun," and the CIA "Stinger."
  4) *Improvised Munitions Handbook: Volumes 1 and 2*, Frankfort Arsenal; reprinted without publisher's name or publication date. These two volumes are taken from the original *Black Book*, described herein.

- Publications from the weapons archives of Canadian John Minnery (including his recent *CIA Catalog of Clandestine Weapons, Tools, and Gadgets*, Paladin Press, Boulder, CO, 1990) contain interesting material from the height of the Cold War.

- CIA Technical Services Staff were drawn from the ranks of audio engineers, locksmiths, and other craftsmen who later saw a post-CIA application for their skills. The close relationships between many private companies manufacturing such equipment began in the 1950s and continued through the 1970s. Audio monitoring devices, originally designed for fighting the Cold War, would later surface, little changed, in commercial catalogs for sale to law enforcement, private investigators, and others during the 1960s and 1970s. Related publications (such as *How to Get Anything On Anybody, Book II: The Encyclopedia of Personal Surveillance*, Lee Lapin, ISECO, San Mateo, CA, 1991) depict equipment that is of CIA origin, or use, e.g., the Fine Wire Kit on page 15, and the Intelligence Case on page 38.

- Foreign publications frequently provide photographs of US espionage equipment:

  1) *Die lautlöse Macht: Geheimdienste nach dem Zweiten Weltkrieg, Book 1*, Verlag Das Beste, Stuttgart, 1985; German; the Dead Drop Device shown herein was pictured on page 316.
  2) *Caught in the Act: Facts About U.S. Espionage and Subversion Against the USSR*, Soviet Information Bureau, Moscow, 1960; Soviet; shown within are the Tear Gas Pen (page 47), RS-6 Transceiver (page 67), and RS-1 Transceiver (page 69, though misidentified as one of its components, the RT-3).

- The collapse of the Soviet Union has resulted in access to files and CIA equipment from a source once unthinkable: the archives and museum of the Second Chief Directorate of the former KGB. A trip to Russia in 1992 provided an opportunity to observe, and identify, a wide array of exhibits showing CIA (and other Western intelligence services) tradecraft equipment from the 1950s and 1960s.

Though the focus of this book is the Cold War period of 1945–1970, some equipment shown may still be in use. Since the necessary requirements of secrecy may forever prevent the officers and technicians of the CIA's Technical Services Staff from receiving personal recognition for their achievements, this book is a tribute to them.

H. Keith Melton

The Founding of the CIA

As World War II ended in 1945, President Truman disbanded the Office of Strategic Services (OSS) as of 1 October by signing Executive Order 9621. The functions of the OSS were transferred to both the State Department and the Department of War.

The head of the OSS, Major General William Donovan, had accurately forecast the need for a centralized intelligence agency in the postwar world. Even prior to the OSS's being disbanded, Gen. Donovan had submitted to President Roosevelt a proposal for a peacetime centralized intelligence service. He called for the creation of a new intelligence organization that would coordinate the intelligence services of several departments, and report to the President. While this new agency would conduct "operations" abroad, it would have no domestic internal security, police, or law enforcement functions.

Quickly feeling the lack of a centralized intelligence service, President Truman set up the Central Intelligence Group (CIG) in January of 1946. Under the authority of the National Intelligence Authority (NIA), it was to coordinate, but not supplant, existing departmental intelligence. Less than two years later the NIA and CIG were deactivated under the provisions of the National Security Act of 1947. In their place the National Security Council (NSC) and Central Intelligence Agency (CIA) were established.

The CIA was charged with two responsibilities that have remained unchanged since 1947. It must first coordinate the numerous intelligence efforts of the US Government, and second collect, evaluate, analyze, produce, and disseminate foreign intelligence. The CIA has become the primary US agency responsible for analysis of intelligence, clandestine HUMINT (Human Intelligence), and covert action. It has also played an important role in the subsequent development of overhead reconnaissance systems, using both aircraft and satellites.

The headquarters of the CIA are located in Langley, Virginia, just outside of Washington, D.C. It also operates technical and training facilities, including the main facility at "The Farm"— Camp Peary, Virginia—and at other locations scattered around the United States.

Entrance to CIA Headquarters at 2430 E Street, Washington, DC. This facility was the headquarters for the CIA from its founding, in 1947, until it moved to its current complex in Langley, Virginia, in late 1961.

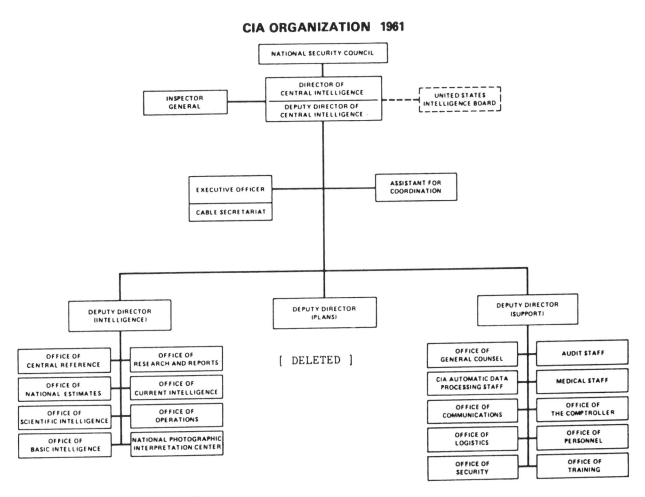

CIA ORGANIZATION 1961

1961 Organizational Chart of the CIA.

Some of the offices from this 1961 organizational chart of the CIA are of special interest:

- **Office of Communications** has responsibility for secret communications between CIA headquarters and overseas installations. It installs, maintains, and operates transmitters and receivers for standard as well as for agent communications.

- **Office of Security** is primarily responsible for the security of CIA facilities and personnel inside and outside the United States. At CIA headquarters, in 1961, uniformed GSA guards were responsible for manning the gates and patrolling the grounds.

- **Office of Training** operates and maintains training facilities, including the main facility at Camp Peary, Virginia. A partial listing of lessons taught for the JOT (Junior Officer Trainee) program to become a CIA Case Officer were:

  - Physical training (including martial arts)
  - Propaganda
  - Infiltration—exfiltration
  - Targeting and penetration of enemy organizations
  - Youth and student organizations
  - Labor operations
  - Liaison operations (with friendly intelligence organizations)
  - Anti-Soviet operations
  - Communist Party penetrations
  - Soviet/Satellite operations
  - Paramilitary operations
  - Agent's handling (individual agents as well as networks)
  - Foreign Intelligence operations (FI)
  - Operational and intelligence reporting

- Intelligence collection methods
- Counterintelligence operations
- Communications
- Codes and ciphers
- Agent recruitment
- Meetings
- Security
- Tradecraft (the tools and techniques used to keep operations secret) and technical skills

- **Technical Services Division (TSD)** was beneath the DDP, or Deputy Director of Plans, and not normally shown on publicly released charts. TSD devised and instructed in methods for secret writing (SW), audio operations (bugging), photography (hidden cameras), flaps and seals (envelope opening), lock picking, and other technical skills. In addition, it trained and stationed experts known as TOPS (Technical Operating Specialists). (In the 1970s, TSD would be relocated to the Directorate of Science and Technology. In 1973, DCI Schlesinger changed the name of DDP to DDO—Deputy Director, Operations.)

The Hon. Allen Welsh Dulles, Director of Central Intelligence from 26 February 1953 to 29 November 1961. (National Archives)

Original CIA Administration Building; former Director of Central Intelligence (DCI) Adm. Hillenkoetter and DCI General Smith had their offices in the lower, right-hand corner of the building. Then-Deputy Director of Plans (DDP) Allen Dulles had his office on the second floor, left-hand window, from January to August 1951.

CIA Special Weapons & Equipment

The CIA Seal

Section 2 of the Central Intelligence Agency Act of 1949 provided for a Seal of Office for the Central Intelligence Agency. The design of the seal was approved and set forth on 17 February 1950 in President Harry S. Truman's Executive Order 10111. In this order, the seal is described in heraldic terms as follows: the Shield—its argent compass rose of 16 points gules; the Crest—on a wreath argent and gules an American Eagle's head erased proper; below the Shield, on a gold scroll, the inscription, "United States of America," in red letters and encircling the Shield and Crest at the top of the inscription, "Central Intelligence Agency" in white letters. All on a circular blue background with a narrow gold edge. The interpretation of the seal—which is characteristic of the Agency itself—is simple and direct. The American bald eagle is the national bird and is the symbol of strength and alertness. The radiating spokes of the compass rose depict the coverage of intelligence data from all areas of the world to a central point.

(from *Intelligence: The Acme of Skill* (CIA Publication, undated)

DEER GUN

DESCRIPTION: The Deer Gun is a 9-mm parabellum, single-shot, reloadable pistol. The receiver is of cast aluminum with a blued steel barrel. It is issued with spare cartridges in the grip, a small instruction manual, and is packed for air drops in a white Styrofoam case.

PURPOSE: The Deer Gun is intended to be distributed in large numbers to friendly personnel in occupied areas. The accompanying instruction sheet is in pictorial form and needs no explanatory text or personal instruction. The weapon's primary purpose is seen in close-proximity, antipersonnel work; it is inaccurate at distances of more than a few yards. Ideally the Deer Gun will be used to take another, but more powerful, weapon from the enemy.

ACTUAL SIZE

Overall length . . . . 5"
Barrel length . . . . 1⅞"
Height . . . . 4¼"
Ammunition . . . . 9-mm parabellum, 3 rounds stored in grip
FSN 1395-H0009108
Official name . . . . Pistol, 9 millimeter
Circa 1967

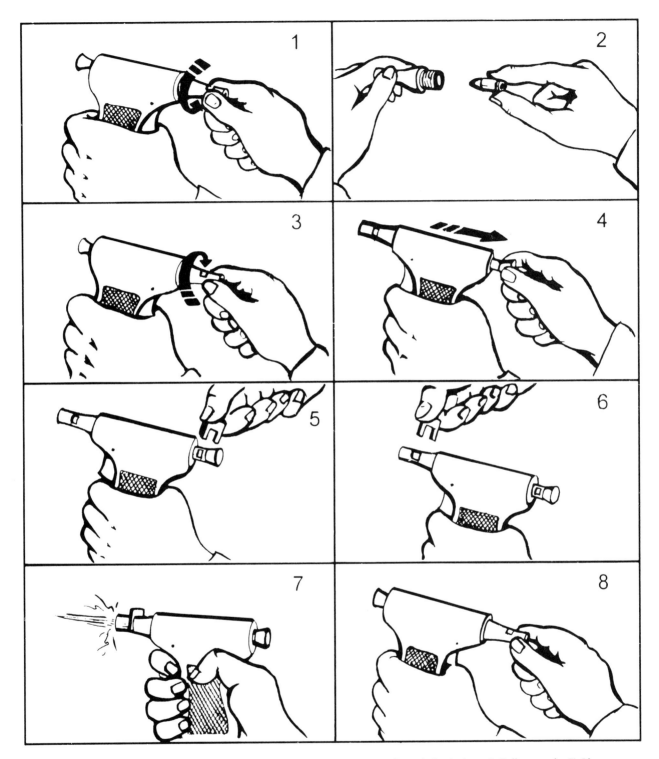

1) Turn barrel counterclockwise to remove; 2) Insert cartridge; 3) Turn barrel clockwise; 4) Pull to cock; 5) Place safety clip in position until ready to fire; 6) Position clip on barrel to serve as front sight; 7) Fire; 8) Repeat unloading procedure.

STINGER

DESCRIPTION: The Stinger is a .22-caliber, reloadable, single-shot weapon. It is issued, with a spare barrel and seven rounds of ammunition, in a camouflaged lead-foil tube.

PURPOSE: The Stinger is an easily concealed .22-caliber gun for short-range one-shot use. Its small size is an advantage for concealment. It can be fired from the palm of the hand at a person sitting in the same room, or passing in a crowd.

ACTUAL SIZE

Overall length . . . . 4½"
Diameter . . . . ¾"
Barrel length . . . . 1¼"
Ammunition . . . . .22 caliber
FSN 1395-H00-0069
Official name . . . . Stinger, .22 Caliber; Reloadable
Circa 1962

Scale = 1 inch

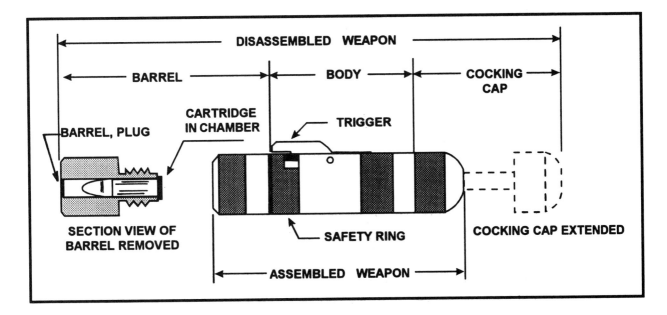

DISASSEMBLED WEAPON

BARREL — BODY — COCKING CAP

BARREL, PLUG

CARTRIDGE IN CHAMBER

TRIGGER

SECTION VIEW OF BARREL REMOVED

SAFETY RING

COCKING CAP EXTENDED

ASSEMBLED WEAPON

General Instructions:

1) DO NOT FIRE OR SNAP weapon without BARREL SCREWED INTO BODY and either a live round or empty CARTRIDGE CASE IN CHAMBER.
2) DO NOT LUBRICATE weapon; weapon has both permanent lubricant and rust-prevention oil sufficient for life of weapon.
3) DO NOT ADJUST any parts in field except safety ring. To change ring tension, remove barrel, pull ring from body, and either open or close ring VERY SLIGHTLY to obtain desired tension.
4) DO NOT BE AFRAID of barrel plugs. Barrels are fitted with tight plugs which blow out easily when weapon is fired.

Operating Instructions:

1) Put safety ring in "FIRE" position by rolling it counter-clockwise to stop.
2) Unscrew cocking cap and draw back until trigger snaps and holds spring load.
3) Return cocking cap and screw tightly onto body, keeping fingers off trigger.
4) Put safety ring in "SAFE" position.
5) Unscrew barrel and remove empty cartridge case.
6) Put new cartridge in chamber and replace barrel.
7) Grasp weapon in hand, trigger under thumb and cocking cap against palm, fingers clear of muzzle.
8) Put safety ring in "FIRE" position with thumb, keeping pressure off trigger.
9) Fire weapon by pressing trigger down firmly with thumb.
10) Repeat operations 2 through 9 to reload and fire.

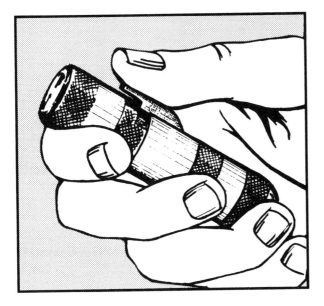

CIGARETTE PISTOL

DESCRIPTION: The Camouflaged Weapon, .22 Caliber, is preloaded for a single shot, and may not be reloaded in the field. It has the same appearance as a standard European king-size cigarette. When concealed in a pack of cigarettes it is indistinguishable.

PURPOSE: The Camouflaged Weapon, .22 Caliber, is produced for use as an "escape and evasion" device when the captive must place his chance of escape on firing one shot. The weapon is intended for use at close range, from actual contact to 10 feet, and is inaccurate at longer distances. Despite its small size, the device has lethal penetrating power equivalent to one and three-quarters inches in soft pine.

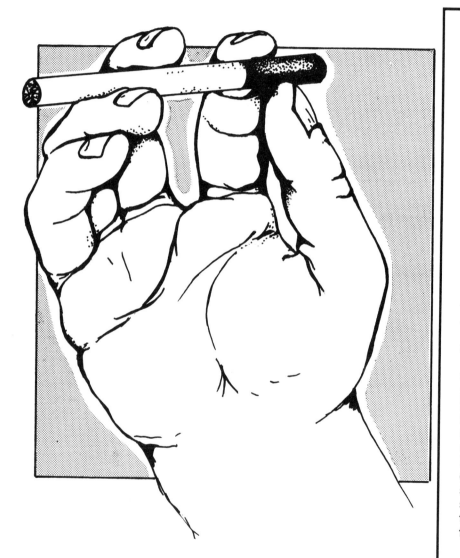

OPERATING INSTRUCTIONS

1. Hold the item as shown in the sketch.

2. Pull safety pin out with your left hand or with your teeth.

3. With the thumb and forefinger, rotate the end *counterclockwise* as far as it will go. The item is now armed and ready to fire.

4. Hold the item so that the end, between your thumb and forefinger, is NOT in line with your body. Push forward with your thumb and forefinger to fire.

CAUTION:

Observe the following precautions to prevent injury to yourself: When fired, the item will recoil out of your hand, but if it is directed away from your body, no jury or discomfort will result. Be sure to hold the item as shown and do not put your thumb over the end to push for firing.

Overall length	2¾"; or identical to standard cigarette in country of intended use
Barrel length	1¼"
Ammunition	.22-caliber, 40-grain bullet
Powder charge	50 mg Bullseye Powder
Muzzle velocity	759 fps
Operating temperature	0–160° F
Official name	Camouflaged Weapon, .22 Caliber; Cigarette
FSN	1395-H00-5670
Circa	1966

DESCRIPTION: The M1903A4 is a special version of the US Rifle Cal. .30 M1903 (Springfield). The rifle has been modified to accept a telescopic sight (Weaver No. 230C, or equivalent) and a Maxim silencer. Adjustment is provided for bringing the cross hairs of the sight and the image of the target into sharp focus.

PURPOSE: Use of the telescopic sight makes it possible for the sniper to get a clear image of a distant target and, by means of the fine adjustment of the cross hairs, place his shot at the exact point on the target desired. The Maxim silencer eliminates the muzzle flash, and substantially reduces the muzzle noise level. The source of the shot is masked, and the location of the weapon firing is difficult for the enemy to locate.

```
Barrel length  . . . . . . . . . . . . . . . . . . . . . . . . . . 24"
Overall length (no silencer)  . . . . . . . . . . . . . . . . . 43½"
Silencer . . . . . . . . . . . Maxim, internal baffle construction
Operation . . . . . . . . . . . . . . . . . . . manual, bolt action
Ammunition  . . .  integral box magazine, 5 rounds, .30 caliber
Weight . . . . . . . . . . . . . . . . . . . . . . . . . . . . . 10 lb
Range . . . . . . . . . . . . . . . . . . . . . 600 yds (effective)
FSN  . . . . . . . 1005-317-2459 (telescopic sight and silencer
                                  must be specified individually)
Official name . . . . . . . . . . . . . Rifle, .30 Caliber; Special
Circa . . . . . . . . . . . . . . . . . . . . . . . . . . . . . . 1947
```

Removable Maxim "Silencer."

ROD PENCIL

DESCRIPTION: The Rod Pencil is a specially modified version of a standard drafting pencil ("KOH-I-NOR" Technigraph 5611-C). Contained within the pen is a 3.3-inch hardened steel shaft that tapers to a needle point. When the end button is depressed, a powerful spring propels the steel shaft forward to the extended position.

PURPOSE: The Rod Pencil is a portable and effectively camouflaged weapon. It is intended for use as an offensive, or defensive, weapon capable of inflicting a lethal wound to the eyes, heart, or other vital body organs.

ACTUAL SIZE

Instructions for Use

1) Hold button in palm of hand with thumb and index finger holding the shaft (like a screwdriver). Push button in all the way (quickly) until the rod snaps out. Release pressure on button immediately to hold rod rigidly. Practice until you are proficient at trapping the rod at full extension.
2) To close, push button and allow rod to drop in on its own momentum. Unless carrying the Rod Pencil for operational use, store with rod extended three-quarters of an inch to protect the spring.
3) Do not compress the rod spring by stabbing tough surfaces.
4) The rod may be disposed of in an emergency by unscrewing the chuck while holding the button depressed and removing the rod and spring. With the rod removed, the pencil is both innocent-appearing and functional for drafting.

Length closed . . . . 5¾"
Length extended . . . . 8⅛"
Official name . . . . Rod Pencil Tech. 5611
(with clip, designated as Rod Pencil Tech. 5611-C)

SILENCED PISTOL KIT

DESCRIPTION: The Silenced Pistol Kit is issued in a small grey hard-sided case of the type used to protect cameras and other optical instruments. Contained within are:

    a) complete sound moderator (in top layer of case);
    b) threaded P-38 barrel assembly (in top layer of case);
    c) rounds of 9-mm Luger, 158-grain full jacket, subsonic ammunition (in bottom layer of case);
    d) bottle-cleaning oil (in bottom layer of case);
    e) pistol-cleaning rod (in bottom layer of case).

PURPOSE: The Silenced Pistol Kit contains a substitute barrel assembly to convert a standard Walther P-38 pistol into a silenced pistol in less than one minute. After use, the P-38 can be returned to its standard configuration with no indication it had been modified. *Any subsequent forensic examination of the pistol would be unable to link it to a bullet fired from the silenced version.* (Care should be taken to ensure that empty cartridge casings are collected and destroyed, since breech face markings *can* be linked to the weapon.)

Using the supplied subsonic ammunition, the modified P-38 pistol is quiet and efficient. The noise at discharge is barely audible over normal conversation, and would be easily masked by a television set or radio playing at normal volume.

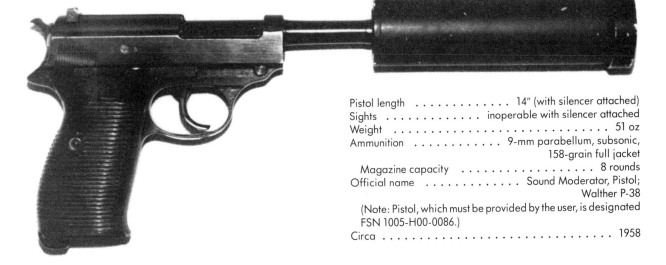

Pistol length . . . . 14″ (with silencer attached)
Sights . . . . inoperable with silencer attached
Weight . . . . 51 oz
Ammunition . . . . 9-mm parabellum, subsonic,
                                   158-grain full jacket
    Magazine capacity . . . . 8 rounds
Official name . . . . Sound Moderator, Pistol;
                                        Walther P-38
(Note: Pistol, which must be provided by the user, is designated FSN 1005-H00-0086.)
Circa 1958

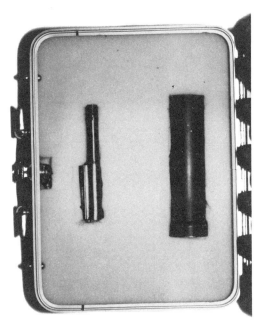

Barrel and Sound Moderator.

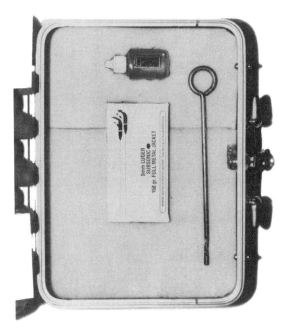

Special Ammunition and Cleaning Tool.

SILENCED RIFLE

DESCRIPTION: The .22-caliber Silenced Rifle is a highly modified version of the Winchester Model-74. The standard barrel on the rifle has been replaced with a one-inch-diameter "bull" barrel that includes an internal silencer.

Length . . . . 40½"
Weight . . . . 7 lb
Ammunition . . . . .22 caliber, subsonic
Magazine capacity . . . . 14 rounds

Official name . . . . Rifle, .22 Caliber, Suppressed;
Winchester Model-74
Circa 1967

PURPOSE: The .22-caliber Silenced Rifle provides operational personnel with a compact, accurate weapon capable of inflicting a lethal wound at ranges up to 100 yards. The internal suppressor is quiet, efficient, and has an extremely low sound signature using special subsonic ammunition. A shot will go unnoticed when masked by normal street noise, a television turned to normal listening volume, or from another room. Its small size (14 inches shorter than the standard silenced Model-74) and conventional appearance make it less conspicuous and easier to transport than the earlier versions of the silenced Model-74. The rifle is not issued with a telescopic sight in order to retain the appearance of a standard commercial rifle. The accuracy produced by the "bull" barrel is sufficient to achieve acceptable accuracy to 100 yards with open iron sights.

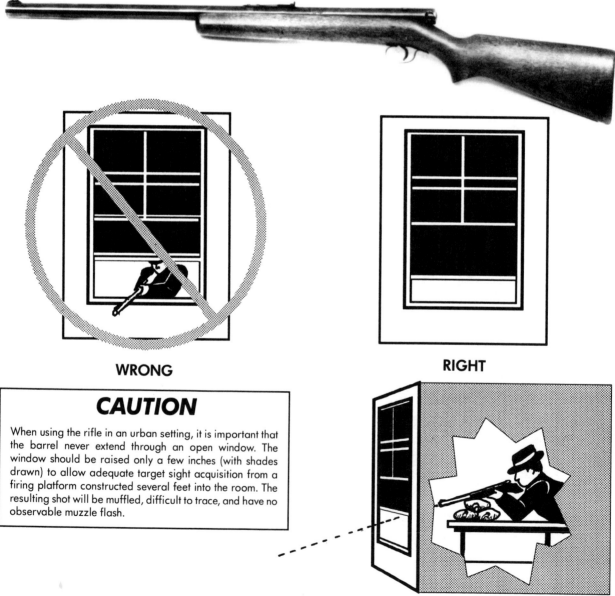

WRONG

RIGHT

CAUTION

When using the rifle in an urban setting, it is important that the barrel never extend through an open window. The window should be raised only a few inches (with shades drawn) to allow adequate target sight acquisition from a firing platform constructed several feet into the room. The resulting shot will be muffled, difficult to trace, and have no observable muzzle flash.

TEAR GAS PEN

DESCRIPTION: The single-shot Tear Gas Pen fires a .38-caliber gas (CS) cartridge. The blued metal barrel and receiver unscrew for reloading. The device is cocked by pulling the knurled ring to the extended position. The "pocket clip" safety slides to the side to allow access to the slightly raised detent ball that serves as its trigger.

PURPOSE: The Tear Gas Pen is a personal gas weapon designed to be carried for defensive purposes in a pocket or purse. The pen has an effective range of six feet and should be fired directly into the face of the target. The tear gas will incapacitate the target long enough to allow an escape. Avoid use of the weapon in any closed area such as an automobile, if at all possible.

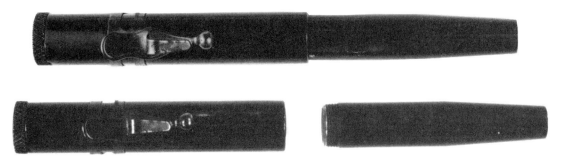

Overall length	5¼"
Barrel length	2"
Caliber	.38-caliber tear gas cartridge
Official name	Weapon, Tear Gas; .38-Caliber Pen
Circa	1948

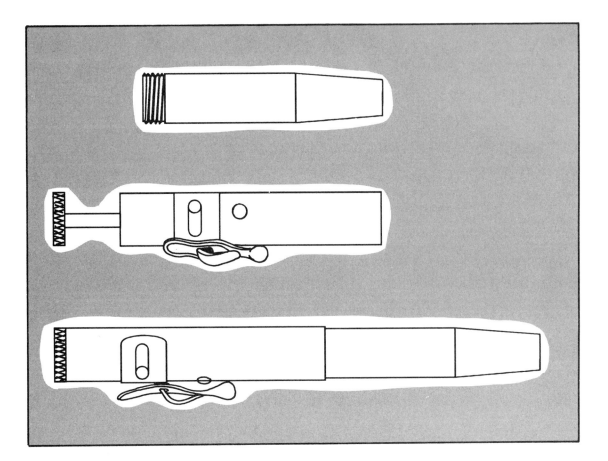

DART GUN

DESCRIPTION: The Dart Gun is a single-shot pistol firing a .03-caliber, mass-stabilized projectile. The tip of the 0.8-inch-long projectile (dart) is made of iron particles and the tranquilizer M-99 formed together with a blood/water-soluble bonding agent. The pistol uses a highly modified, electrically detonated cartridge. The small dart is fired through a sound-suppressed (integral silencer) hypodermic-needle-quality barrel with a .033 bore. The pistol comes preloaded, and can be reloaded in the field by unscrewing the end cap. The dart is prevented from slipping from the cartridge by a grease dab.

The all-metal pistol is fitted with a 1.3× telescopic sight that has been presighted at the factory.

PURPOSE: The Dart Gun is used for quieting (tranquilizing) guard dogs and other animals. The fired dart enters the skin of the target at such a high speed, and with such a small diameter, that it is often ignored, or misperceived as an insect bite. If left in the body, the dart dissolves and becomes unidentifiable on X ray. Depending on the size of the animal, the tranquilizer will take effect in about 15 minutes. The target will remain unconscious for approximately 30 minutes, with the only aftereffect being grogginess. If the target is to be revived after a short interval, an antidote of 5 mg of Nalorphine Hydrochloride should be administered intramuscularly.

Cartridge . . . . modified
Dart . . . . 0.8" length; mass stabilized
Ammunition . . . . .03 caliber
Scope . . . . Bushnel, 1.3×; field of view 16–18 ft at 100 yds; eye relief from 6" to 21"
Ignition . . . . electric
Official name . . . . Bio-inoculator
Circa 1966
Issued by . . . . Army Security Agency

The Dart Gun has an effective range of 50 feet. The low sound signature of the device allows it to be used safely in a variety of operational applications. An adjustable shoulder stock is available as an accessory (must be obtained separately) for operations requiring shots at ranges up to 100 feet.

WALTHER PPK SILENCED PISTOL

DESCRIPTION: The Walther PPK Silenced Pistol is a specially modified version of the standard PPK. The model PP barrel has been threaded to accept a leather-covered double-chambered suppressor (silencer) of European design. Both the upper and lower chamber of the suppressor have end caps that allow for disassembly and cleaning.

PURPOSE: The Walther PPK Silenced Pistol is a small but powerful weapon that can be easily separated into two components (pistol and silencer) for carrying and concealment. The unique design of the suppressor provides a second chamber beneath the barrel to receive and cool the muzzle gases upon firing. This design is not only efficient, but also allows the utilization of the existing open sights on the PPK. Using subsonic ammunition, the special PPK pistol is quiet and accurate.

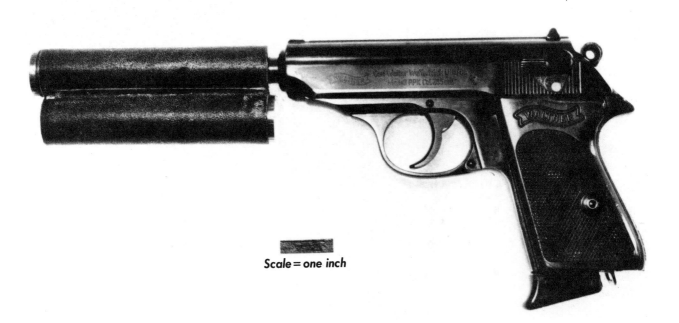

Scale = one inch

Pistol length	6¼"
Silencer length	4½"
Sights	open
Weight	22 oz (excluding silencer)
Ammunition	7.65 mm, subsonic (must be obtained separately)
Magazine capacity	7 rounds
Official name	Pistol, Walther PPK; Suppressed
FSN	1005-H00-0290
Circa	1951

PHOTOGRAPHERS

CIA . . . where you can develop an exciting career

If you're a Photographer with a degree or an extensive background in technical, scientific, intelligence-related or remote sensing photography, you can develop an exciting career with the National Photographic Interpretation Center (NPIC). NPIC, an office of the Central Intelligence Agency, seeks talented photographers to work in a custom photographic laboratory.

These challenging positions require more than job-related knowledge . . . they require a high degree of dedication and professionalism. You'll work with experienced professionals on the latest processors, printers and densitometers, and plan and organize photographic coverage for a variety of assignments, including studio and video work. This position also includes darkroom work and operation of standard as well as highly specialized cameras and enlargers.

If you are a U.S. citizen and can meet our security requirements, you may qualify for this unique career in photography. All positions are in the Washington, D.C. area, in modern facilities featuring state-of-the-art equipment and technology. Salary is commensurate with education and experience. If you qualify for this exciting career with NPIC, please send your resume to:

Central Intelligence Agency
Building 213
NPIC/Personnel (E45)
Washington, D.C. 20505

An equal opportunity/affirmative action employer.

Post-Cold War recruiting ad placed by the CIA.

DESCRIPTION: The Minox, Model-B is the central component of a highly efficient camera system.

Body .... anodized aluminum available in satin silver or black finish
Lens .... 15-mm 4-element Complan anastigmat with full aperture
Focusing range .... from 8" (20 cm) to infinity
Exposure metering .... built-in photoelectric (selenium) cell
Length .... 3⅝" (9.8 cm)
Width .... 1" (2.8 cm)
Height .... ¾" (1.6 cm)
Weight .... 3.25 oz (92 grams)
Filters .... moveable (internal) grey or green
Negative size ... 8 mm × 11 mm on a 50-exposure cassette
Flash synch. .... yes, ½₀₀ sec for electronic flash, ½₀ sec for flash bulbs
Shutter speeds ..... from ½ to ⅟₁₀₀₀ sec, plus B & T settings

PURPOSE: The Minox, Model-B camera system offers the advantages of a precision photographic instrument that is small enough to be hidden in a closed fist. It is easy to conceal and unobtrusive to use.

Film .... a wide assortment of films are available including standard black and white, as well as infrared and color
Case ..... issued with standard case and measuring chain

ACTUAL SIZE

Accessories .... flash units, either electronic or bulb
.... copying stand
.... binocular attachment
.... tripod head
.... pocket tripod
.... right-angle mirror finder
.... developing tank
.... film-viewing magnifier
.... Minox enlarger
.... Minox projector

Official name .... Camera, Subminiature; Minox, Model-B
Circa 1958

Steady the Minox against your face,

tuck both elbows well into your side,

and stand with your feet slightly apart.

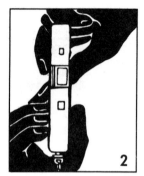

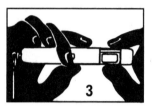

1) Right; 2) Right; 3) WRONG: Don't allow finger to cover lens.

CAMERA HELD BEHIND OPEN FOLD OF COAT

COAT POCKET

SUB-MINIATURE CAMERA

SPECIALLY DESIGNED SLOT IN POCKET WITH A LENS TUBE FOR PENETRATING IT WHEN NEEDED.

SUB-MINIATURE CAMERA IN FOLD OF GLOVES

CAMERA HELD IN POCKET

ACTUAL SIZE

Binocular adapter clamp.

Using the accessories available (either measuring chain or copy stand), it can focus as close as eight and one-half inches for copying documents or photographs. It is effective for surveillance photographs, as well as for recording buildings, bridges, airfields, or military equipment. When used with binoculars (accessory attachment) it is suitable for taking photographs over extended distances.

The Model-B has replaced the older Model-A and is preferred over the newer Model-C because its photoelectric exposure meter does not require a battery; the selenium cell is powered by ambient light. For this reason the Model-B may be efficiently stored for long periods of time. It is also desirable for use in areas in which replacement batteries are unavailable.

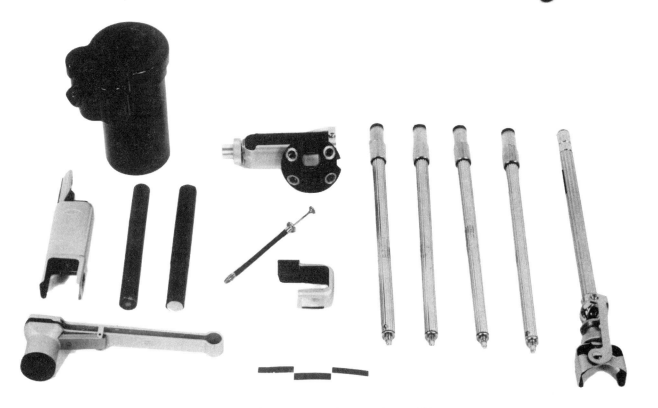

Minox Intelligence Kit with special accessories for document photography and film processing.

CIGARETTE LIGHTER CAMERA

DESCRIPTION: The Cigarette Lighter Camera, Echo-8, is a small photographic device concealed inside a standard "Zippo"-style lighter. The camera is fitted into the case with a working fluid lighter. The solidly machined film slitter allows film to be sized for the camera using any available Cine-film stock. The Echo-8 is issued with a spare film magazine and film slitter.

PURPOSE: The Echo-8 Cigarette Lighter Camera is the smallest camera commercially produced. It is a highly effective concealment camera for surveillance photography. It is suitable for photographing individuals, and may be used safely in both business and social settings, as well as in public. If necessary, it can be used for lighting a cigarette. For surveillance work the camera should be aimed instinctively. For best results, several practice rolls should be taken. With the optional close-up lens, the camera can be used for document photography.

ACTUAL SIZE

Lens . . . . Echor Anastigmat F = 15 mm, 1:3.5
Iris 1:3.5: 5:6-8
Shutter . . . . B-1/50 sec
Film . . . . 16-mm Cine-film, half-cut size
Exposures . . . . 20 exposures from 8"-length
film using a magazine

Length . . . . 1 5/8"
Width . . . . 7/16"
Height . . . . 2 1/4"
Weight . . . . 5 3/4 oz
Accessories . . . . filters and close-up lens with focusing to 8"
Official name . . . . Camera, Cigarette Lighter
Circa 1951

"Echo 8"

Camera & Lighter Combination

INSTRUCTIONS OF HOW TO USE "ECHO-8"

FEATURES:

Lens   : Echor Anastigmat F=15mm 1 : 3.5

Iris   : 1 : 3.5. 5.6-8

Shutter : B-1/50

Film   : 16mm Cine-film, half cut size

Exposures : 20 exposures from 8 inches length film
using a magazine

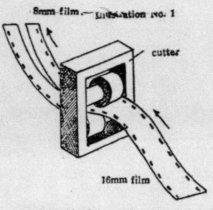

8mm film.— Illustration No. 1

cutter

16mm film

1   HOW TO PLACE FILM INTO MAGAZINE:

A. Cut 16 mm Cine-film to the length af 8 inches.

B. Put 16 mm film through Film Cutter to split into half
width size. (Illustration # 1)

C. Keep the film perforation downward to wind film to
the spool ot magazine. It is important that one end
is just slided into the Spring Band of fhe spool. so it
will slip off at the last exposure. (Illustration # 2)

D. Next step is to attach the other end to the Winding
Spool or Gsar and set into the magaine. Bend 2 mm
of fimm and hook the end to the Spring Band, so the
film will not slip 0ff when winding. (Ill ustratifn #3)

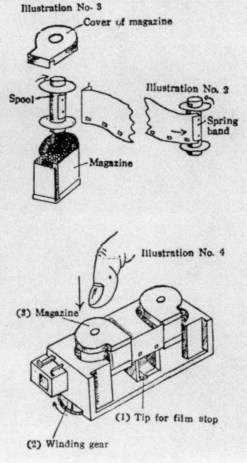

Illustration No. 3

Cover of magazine

Spool

Magazine

Illustration No. 2

Spring band

2   HOW TO FIX THE FILM(MAGAZINE) INTO THE BODY OF CAMERA :

A. As shown on Illustratiton #4, place magazine containing
film (Illustratiton # 4) into the body revolving film
winder or Gear(#2). It is important that both magazine
are completely set into the body.

B. Film must be centered and firmly on the body. Wind
film until Tip (# 1) fits the perforation to stop the
winding. (Illustralon #4)

3   PREPARATION FOR SHOOTING :

After the film is completely placed into the body, take
2 trial shots rolling just 1 cut of film. The trial shots
were taken as the first cut of film is already exposed

Illustration No. 4

(3) Magazine

(2) Winding gear

(1) Tip for film stop

WRISTWATCH CAMERA

DESCRIPTION: The Steineck ABC Camera is a miniature photographic device built to the size and appearance of an ordinary man's wristwatch. It uses circular cut film 25 mm in diameter and produces six exposures in 6-mm-diameter format. The small lens is f2.5, fixed focus, with a shutter speed of ¹⁄₅₀ sec.

PURPOSE: The Steineck ABC is worn as a wristwatch. It provides the wearer with a ready camera for surveillance photography. Taking a photograph with the Steineck is as natural, and unobtrusive, as checking the time. Best results will be obtained with practice.

ACTUAL SIZE

Length . . . . 1¾" (excluding band)
Width . . . . 1⅜" (excluding band)
Height . . . . ⅞" (excluding band)
Official name . . . . Camera, Wristwatch; Steineck ABC
Circa 1949

DESCRIPTION: The Agent Camera is a specially constructed photographic device in a cylindrical, black case only slightly larger than a standard 35-mm film cassette. The film is advanced manually by a counter-clockwise rotation of the body. The shutter is cocked by a clockwise rotation of the shutter release knob, and is released by depressing the same knob.

PURPOSE: The Agent Camera is a highly miniaturized photographic instrument designed to copy documents, drawings, and photographs with a maximum diagonal measurement of 36 cm. The camera is prefocused at 28 cm; a small measuring chain is provided to quickly gauge the correct distance. The exposure setting is preset and fixed for indoor photography using available light. The camera uses a special black-and-white film with sufficient exposure latitude to compensate for a wide variety of lighting conditions. The camera is dependable to use, simple to operate, and produces high-quality document copies.

Camera	special
Lens	preset
Shutter	preset
Official name	Camera, Document Copy; Special

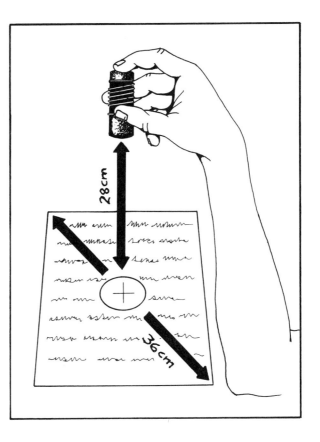

SURVEILLANCE CAMERA

DESCRIPTION: The Surveillance Camera is a Nikon 35-mm Model-F camera fitted with a 250-exposure film back, and F250 motor drive. This high-quality photographic instrument uses an 85- to 250-mm f:4 Nikkor zoom lens. The remote control unit is the Nikon Radio Control Set MW-1.

PURPOSE: The Surveillance Camera is designed to take surveillance photographs, unattended, of persons who pass through a beam, or otherwise trigger the Remote Radio Control Set. A typical application of the system would be to photograph persons entering or exiting a doorway at a foreign embassy or other location under surveillance. This system, after installation and testing, can operate unattended other than for regular film unloading and reloading. Exposure adjustments must be made as required to compensate for significant variations in available light.

Camera . . . . Nikon Model-F; 35 mm
Lens . . . . Nikkor 85 to 250, f:4 zoom
Shutter . . . . T, B to ¹⁄₁₀₀₀ sec
Remote . . . . Nikon MW-1 with telescopic sensor
Official name . . . . Camera Set, Still Picture, 35-mm;
Nikon F250; Special
Circa 1969

The proper use of the system will result in sharp, clear photographs to aid in the visual recognition and/or identification of the subject(s) under surveillance.

Camera is concealed behind one-way glass.

DESCRIPTION: The Cigarette Pack Camera is a Tessina 35-mm, SLR camera fitted inside a modified pack of cigarettes. The cigarette pack (box) has been reinforced with a metal shell to accommodate the camera. The photograph is taken through small perforations on the side of the pack.

ACTUAL SIZE

PURPOSE: The Cigarette Pack Camera is a precision photographic instrument effectively concealed within a standard cigarette pack (box). The photograph is taken by pressing the shutter release through the side of the pack. An internal spring-wound motor allows for one to ten shots to be taken before rewinding. A special model (shown here) is fitted with nylon gears to effectively silence the film advance.

The Cigarette Pack Camera is ideal for surveillance photographs of individuals at close distances. The photographs taken with the Tessina can, optimally, compare with high-quality 35-mm photographs taken by full-size SLR cameras.

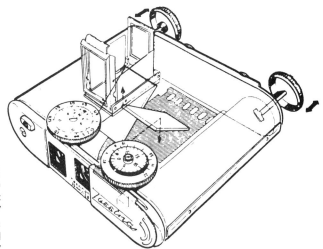

Camera . . . . Tessina, 35-mm (silent operation)
Lens . . . . Tessinon, f:2.8, 25-mm
Shutter . . . . ½ to ¹⁄₅₀₀ sec
Camera dimensions . . . . 2¾″ × 2¼″ × 1¹⁄₁₆″
Official name . . . . Camera, Cigarette Pack, 35-mm;
Tessina; Special
Circa 1967

SECRET WRITING

PURPOSE: Secret Writing (SW) is a means of communications that causes a message to be hidden, or invisible, on an innocent-appearing letter or cover document.

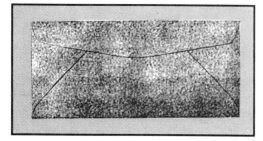

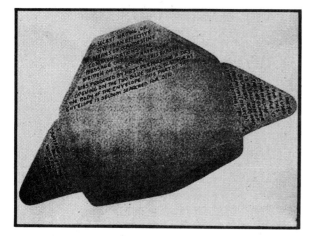

DESCRIPTION: Three basic types of systems of SW are in use:

Wet Systems: These systems use chemicals, usually disguised as pills, or impregnated in a common-appearing handkerchief, sock, or scarf, that are dissolved in water to create a special ink. The message is written (preferably printed) with the special ink on good-quality bond paper with a wooden stylus, and is invisible upon drying. Care must be taken to avoid damaging the fibres of the paper with excess writing pressure, since the disturbed fibres may alert postal censors to the possibility of a hidden message. After writing, the paper is sized by rubbing with a soft cloth in all four directions to further disguise the presence of a message. The paper is then lightly steamed and pressed within a thick book to dry. Afterwards it is tested for any visual signs of the message, as well as given an inspection under an ultraviolet light. When complete, a cover letter, or innocent-appearing message is written on the paper in regular ink, on top of the invisible message.

Carbon System: The carbon system consists of special sheets of dry white bond paper that have been impregnated with SW chemicals. A plain sheet of bond paper is placed on top of, and beneath, the impregnated "carbon" sheet. A message is written in pencil on the top sheet applying the proper pressure. The chemical in the impregnated "carbon" is transferred to the bottom sheet with minimal damage to the fibres of the paper. The cover message is then written on the reverse side of the sheet from the secret message. Upon completion, both the original and "carbon" sheet are destroyed for security considerations.

On receipt of the SW letter, the agent applies the proper reagent (chemical developer) with a cotton swab to make the hidden message appear. As soon as it appears, the document is quickly photographed to preserve the hidden message in a photographic image.

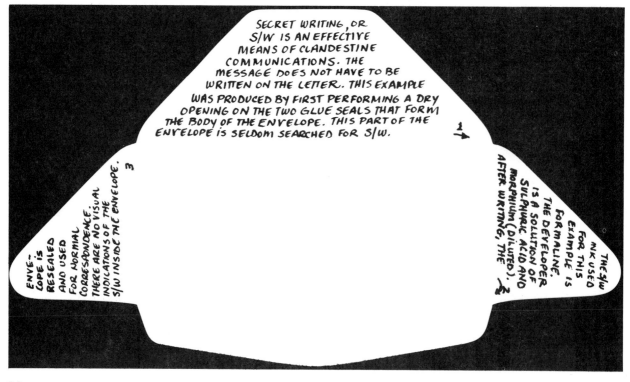

Microdots: A microdot is a small piece of photographic film, about the size of the period following this sentence, that contains a written message. The message is invisible to the unaided eye, and may only be read with a microscope or other type of optical magnifier.

A special camera kit has been developed that allows a standard-size document to be reduced to that of a microdot in a single step. Instructions are also provided that allow microdots to be produced in a two-step process using a conventional 35-mm camera, together with a subminiature camera, such as the Minox. Special Kodak 649F spectrographic stripping film is the standard for the production of microdots.

In practice, the microdot is hidden, or "buried," within a cover document of innocent appearance. Microdots must be "buried" precisely in a previously agreed-upon location so they may be found and viewed. The microdot is a very secure means of sending secret messages.

1

2

1) Concealable microdot viewer; 2) Pocket-size microdot microscope; 3) Special equipment for reading and producing microdots.

ACTUAL SIZE

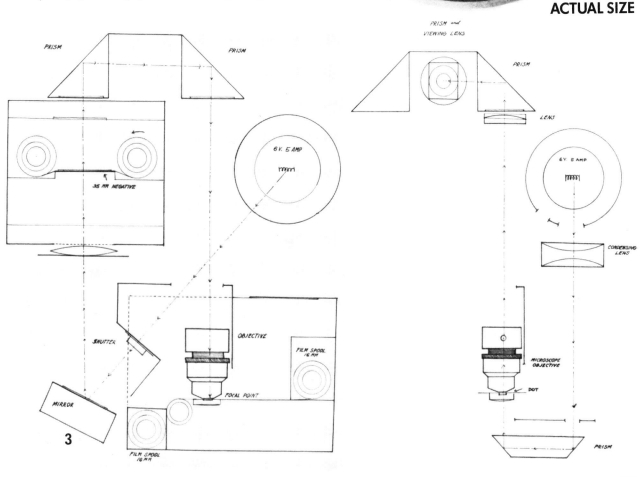

METASCOPE

DESCRIPTION: The Metascope is a small, hand-held, battery-operated infrared detecting device. It consists of a detachable infrared light source, carrying strap, infrared image-forming receiver, and a carrying case equipped with belt hooks.

PURPOSE: The Metascope was originally designed for use on the battlefield in spotting enemy infrared emissions. It is an easily concealed and portable infrared viewer (passive receiver) with applications off the battlefield as well.

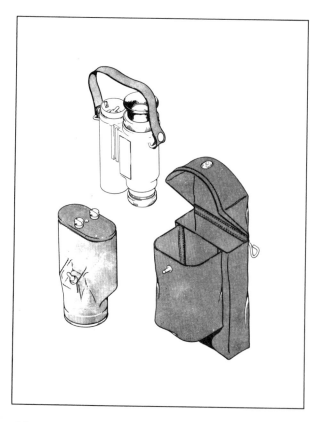

It is ideally suited for situations in which the presence of a visible light source would be compromising. Combined with a small portable infrared light source (such as taping an infrared filter over the lens of an ordinary flashlight), it offers the ability to search a target room in near darkness. The dull red glow given off by a small infrared light source is nearly invisible at distances greater than a few feet. Using this viewer, it is possible to read documents and conduct effective searches without the presence of visible (to the unaided eye) light.

The Metascope should be used to scan a dark room prior to entering so as to detect the presence of any hidden infrared beams that may be part of the target's security system.

Warning: Never point the Metascope towards the sun, or any other intense light source.

Overall length	6"
Overall height	4½"
Overall width	4½"
Overall weight	2 lb 12 oz
Model	No. 9902A
Magnification	1.1
Range	12" to infinity
Field of view	26° minimum
Power	1.34-V dry cell (BA1321U)
Light source	any infrared source
REF	TM 5-1090-203-15
Official name	Metascope Assembly, Image, Infrared, Transistorized
FSN	1090-790-6197

INFRARED FLASH PHOTOGRAPHY

DESCRIPTION: The standard commercial flash unit shown has been readily modified by taping an infrared filter (or Kodak Wratten gelatin filters nos. 87, 87C, 88A, or 89B) over the lens of the flash. The camera is loaded with Kodak high-speed infrared film 2481 (Estar Base).

PURPOSE: High-speed infrared photography allows photographs to be successfully taken in near darkness using infrared flash. It is possible to operate in total darkness and take flash photographs that are invisible to the unaided human eye. When developed, the resulting images may be printed on standard black-and-white photographic paper.

Infrared flash photography has many possible applications where operational circumstances do not allow the use of light in the visible spectrum, including:

a) recording the interior and contents of an office following an entry;
b) copying documents that may not be removed during an entry;
c) photographing wall maps, organizational charts, etc., that are discovered during an entry; and
d) specialized surveillance photography in unusual low-light situations.

Technical Note: Infrared film has unique properties that differentiate it from conventional black-and-white films. Prior to operational use, care must be taken to establish effective exposure times, focusing methods, and development procedures. (For an initial estimate of exposure time, start six stops above normal, and then bracket until acceptable results are achieved.)

Color sensitivity .. through the visible regions of the spectrum, and in the infrared to approximately 900 nm with maximum sensitivity from 770 nm to 840 nm

Safelight ...... total darkness required during loading and processing

Storage .... unexposed film should be kept in a refrigerator or freezer at 13 °C (55 °F).

Exposed film .... process as soon as possible; if processing must be delayed, reseal film and refrigerate below 40 °F

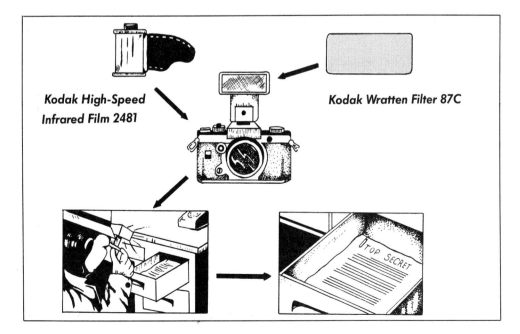

Kodak High-Speed Infrared Film 2481

Kodak Wratten Filter 87C

ROBOT CAMERA

DESCRIPTION: The Robot Camera is a 35-mm Robot Star II concealed inside a suede waist belt. The camera takes the photograph through a false button, or man's tie clip, affixed to the front of the lens. The shutter is tripped by a remote cable release running from the camera to the coat pocket of the user.

PURPOSE: The Robot Camera is designed for taking surveillance photographs of people and meetings. The camera is worn in the waist belt so that:

a) only the false button protrudes through the user's closed coat. A spare set of buttons (in three different sizes) is issued with the camera so that all buttons on the user's coat will be matching; or

b) it is mated to a specially designed tie clip that allows photographs to be taken through the tie.

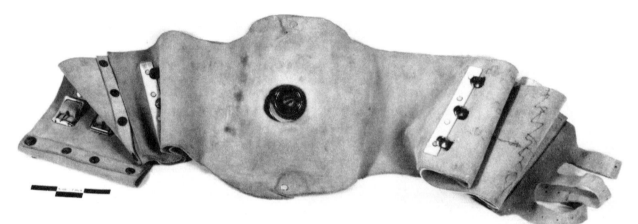

Robot Camera with buttonhole lens mounted in waist belt.

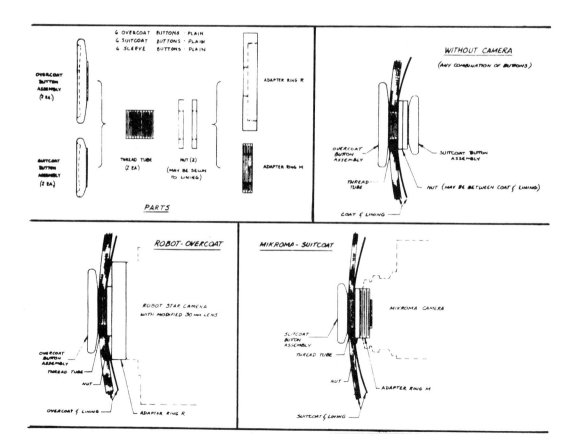

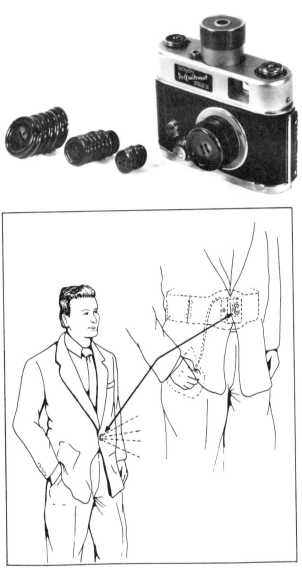

Robot Camera with false button mounted over lens.

The Robot Star II camera uses a spring-motor film advance. It is manually wound, prior to insertion into the portfolio case, using the large knob protruding from the top of the camera. A roll of 24 exposures can be taken without rewinding. Any camera noises are effectively muffled by the waist belt and coat.

Waist belt . . . . 40", plus 11" of strap adjustment
Weight . . . . 3 lb
Camera . . . . Robot Star II
Lens . . . . f:3.5; false button, or tie clip, and special lens mounted on a threaded adapter screws into the camera in replacement of the standard Radionar lens
Depth of field . . from 19 ft to infinity using lens provided; a special washer is provided to be mounted on the back of the lens that will give an acceptable depth of field from 5½ ft to 11 ft
Shutter speed . . . . ¼ to ¹⁄₅₀₀ sec plus "B"
Film . . . . 35-mm, Kodak Tri-X black-and-white film
Official name . . . . Camera, Concealed; Waist Belt
Circa 1965

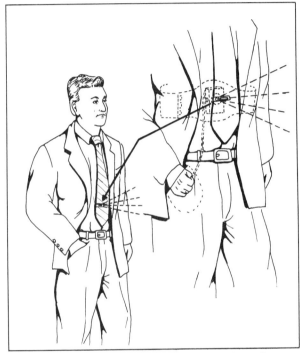

Robot Camera with lens mounted on "see-through" tie clip.

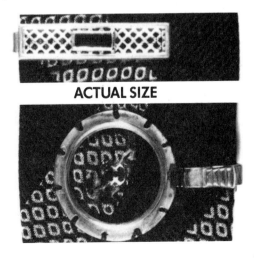

ACTUAL SIZE

TECHNICAL INTELLIGENCE FIELD KIT

DESCRIPTION: The Technical Intelligence Field Kit is contained within Leica Universal Carrying Case (No. 14,803). It has the following components:

a) Leica M-3 camera, 35 mm;
b) Leitz Summicron lens; f2, 50 mm;
c) Leitz Elmar lens; f4, 135 mm;
d) Leitz Summaron lens; f2.8, 35mm;
e) Leica flash unit CEYOO; and
f) spare cassettes and spools are stored in the front side-pocket.

PURPOSE: The Technical Intelligence Field Kit provides its user with the ability to collect and record detailed, documentary information in a quick, timely, and efficient manner. Anything of possible military use, significance, or importance is a suitable subject for intelligence photography.

The equipment contained in the kit provides a basic assortment of photographic tools for intelligence collection. To use this equipment effectively and efficiently requires a basic knowledge of photography and an in-depth familiarity with the items. Additional accessories are available for other specialized photographic tasks.

Case dimensions .... 11" × 5½" × 7"	Flash .... Leica CEYOO
Camera .... Leica M-3, 35-mm	Official name .. Camera Set, Still Picture, 35-mm, KS-15 (3)
Lens .... 35 mm, 50 mm, and 135 mm	FSN 6760-823-9699
Shutter .... B to ¹⁄₁₀₀₀ sec	Circa 1955

SHOOT THRU WINDOW AND DRIVE AS SLOWLY AS POSSIBLE.

DO NOT REST ELBOWS ON ANY PART OF CAR.

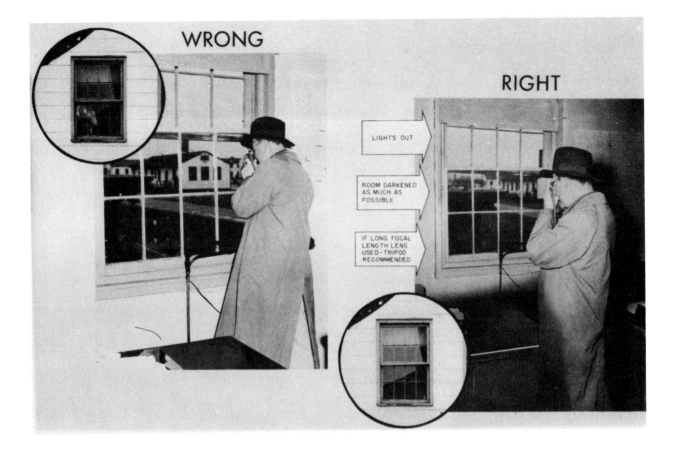

WRONG

RIGHT

LIGHTS OUT

ROOM DARKENED AS MUCH AS POSSIBLE

IF LONG FOCAL LENGTH LENS USED—TRIPOD RECOMMENDED

WINDOW OPEN IF POSSIBLE

SUBJECT: AIRCRAFT OR MISSILE ON FLAT CAR

ELBOWS SNUGLY AGAINST SIDES - MUST NOT REST AGAINST ANY PART OF TRAIN

KNEES BENT AND LEGS SLIGHTLY APART

HEEL OFF THE FLOOR

HIDDEN CAMERA

DESCRIPTION: The Hidden Camera is a 35-mm Robot Star II concealed inside a brown leather portfolio case. The photograph is taken by pressing on the outside of the case (at the designated spot) to trip the lever-actuated shutter release.

PURPOSE: The Hidden Camera is designed for taking clandestine photographs of people, meetings, buildings, vehicles, etc. When the portfolio is carried in the position shown, photographs are taken at a 90-degree angle to the user; sighting is instinctive. In advance of any operational use, several practice rolls of film should be taken to develop this technique.

The Robot Star II camera uses a spring-motor film advance. It is manually wound, prior to insertion into the portfolio case, using the large knob protruding from the top of the camera. A roll of 24 exposures can be taken without opening the portfolio case. Any camera noises are effectively muffled by the case.

Camera can be adapted for mounting in different-style briefcases to match those in use within the target country.

Case dimensions . . . . 12″ × 16½″ × 3″
Weight . . . . 5 lb
Camera . . . . Robot Star II
Lens . . . . Radionar; f:3.5, 38 mm
Shutter speed . . . . ¼ to ⅟₅₀₀ sec plus "B"
Film . . . . 35-mm, Kodak Tri-X black-and-white film
Official name . . . . Camera, Concealed; Portfolio Case
Circa 1965

DOCUMENT-COPYING ATTACHÉ CASE

DESCRIPTION: The standard attaché case contains a fitted document copy stand, camera, and lights. There is no external modification of the case to alter its ordinary appearance. Within the case are:

a) aluminum frame and support with base;
b) swing-out copy lights;
c) power pack providing 110- and 220-V AC, and 90-V battery;
d) Honeywell Pentax SL camera, 35-mm; and
e) remote shutter release.

PURPOSE: The document-copying device collapses into an attaché case for storage and travel. When assembled, it presents a one-position copy device complete with lighting which accepts originals to a maximum of nine inches by fourteen inches. The Pentax camera has been modified for fixed focus, selected aperture (f/11), and silent operation. As long as the shutter is set at ¹⁄₁₅ second, the copy setup will produce properly exposed and focused negatives.

Film and Processing: For document copying or photography of flat objects, the following are recommended:

Film . . . . Kodak Panatomic-X; 35 mm
Exposure . . . . ¹⁄₁₅ sec
Developer . . . . Kodak Dektol diluted 1:1 for six minutes at 68° F for document copy. Kodak D-76 diluted 1:1 for nine minutes at 68° F for other photography

Case dimensions . . . . 18″ × 12″ × 4½″
Weight . . . . 19 lb
Battery . . . . 90-V Eveready #479, or equivalent (NEDA 214)
Lamps . . . . 28-V G.E. 304
Official name . . . . Document-Copying Kit, Mark III
Circa 1968

FIBERSCOPE

DESCRIPTION: The Fiberscope is composed of the pistol-grip viewer and a flexible shaft. Within the shaft are two separate fibre-optic bundles. The "image" bundle contains 7500 fibres carefully arranged so that each fibre is in the same relative position at either end of the bundle. The illuminating halo surrounds the image bundle and carries light from the lamp in the handle to the viewing area. The image is illuminated (adjustable) from the internal lamp and transmitted through the image bundle to the other end of the Fiberscope, where a 10× eyepiece magnifies the image for viewing.

PURPOSE: The fiberscope is designed to visually inspect remote or inaccessible locations. It may be used for:

a) conducting undetected surveillance of a target room after drilling a 0.315 inch hole for the Fiberscope tip in the wall or ceiling, or by sliding the tip beneath the target's doorway. It can aid in determining whether a room is empty or occupied before an entry;
b) as a technical tool for use when drilling microphone or transmitter holes in a target wall. The Fiberscope allows an internal examination of the construction materials being encountered in the walls, and examination of hollow spaces or obstructions that may be encountered.

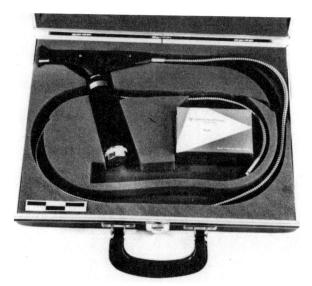

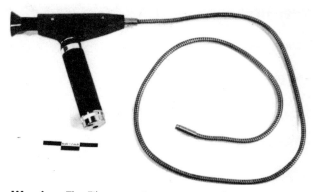

Warning: The Fiberscope is not waterproof and may not be submerged. Clean only with a mixture of 70 percent alcohol.

Field of view . . . . 60° fixed focus
Flexible length of probe . . . . 48"

Magnification . . . . 10× internal
Maximum diameter of probe . . . . 0.315"
Depth of focus . . . . ¾" to infinity
Radius of bend . . . . 1¾" minimum inside
Power . . . . two 1.5-V "C" cells
Light source . . . . internal lamp (Model 11495)
Model . . . . No. FS-100
Accessory (included) . . . . right-angle viewing mirror
Official name . . . . Fiberscope, FS-100
Circa 1969

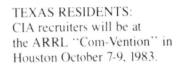
Cold War recruiting ad placed by the CIA.

RADIO STATION; RS-1

DESCRIPTION: The RS-1 is a portable shortwave radio station in four waterproof containers suitable for most climatic conditions and for long periods of storage before use. The set operates in the frequency range 3–22 MHz (transmit), 3–24 MHz (receive), sending CW (Morse) and receiving CW and AM (telephony).

It comprises four units, operating from AC mains or six-volt car-type battery:
  a) radio transmitter, RT-3;
  b) radio receiver, RR-2;
  c) power supply, RP-1 or RP-2; and
  d) spares/accessory kit (standard issue).

PURPOSE: The RS-1 is a rugged, portable radio station intended for use in harsh terrain. It is ideally suited for use by operational forces and intelligence personnel needing clandestine communication equipment capable of operating from a variety of energy sources. The operational range of the RS-1 is dependent on the frequency used, time of day, season, and atmospheric conditions. Under optimum operating conditions it has a range of 3000 miles.

Power Unit RP-1: operates from AC supplies between 76 and 260 V, and 40 to 400 Hz, or from a heavy-duty 6-V battery. A 0- to 300-V meter checks the AC mains to ensure correct setting, and fuses protect the AC and 6-V inputs. It provides regulated 1.3 V and 100 V for the receiver and 6 V and 400 V for the transmitter, and can also supply 3 to 4 amps. for recharging a 6-V battery. Provision is made for connection of the Hand-Cranked Generator, Type SSP-11, when no mains or battery supply is available. The power unit RP-2 is as RP-1, but for AC input only. The receiver may be used separately from dry batteries, 1.5-V "A" and 90-V "B."

Transmitter: 3 to 22 MHz in 4 bands, RF power 10 to 15 watts, with break-in keying and matching to open-wire random-length antennas: 8⅝" × 5½" × 5⁷⁄₁₆", 9 lb.

Receiver: 3 to 24 MHz in 3 bands : sensitivity 1.5 micro V for 10 dB S/N ratio. Selectivity 8 kHz at 20 dB down, 15 kHz at 40 dB down, with image ratio 35 dB at 24 MHz and 60 dB at 3 MHz. 1800 division dial with frequency calibration less than 0.08%. The BFO is variable +/−4 kHz from center IF of 455 kHz. The transmitter frequency is controlled by plug-in quartz crystals. The receiver may be continuously tuned or crystal-controlled for fixed-frequency (spot) operation. Size same as Transmitter weight 10 lb.

Weight . . . . . . complete station, less 6-V AC, with RP-1, 40 lb; with RP-2, 55 lb
Official name . . . . Radio Station, Portable; Type RS-1
Circa 1950

DESCRIPTION: The RS-6 comprises four units in sturdy metal cases, plus a plastic pouch for antenna parts:

   a) transmitter, RT-6;
   b) receiver, RR-6;
   c) power supply, RP-6; and
   d) filter and accessory unit, RA-6.

PURPOSE: The RS-6 is a portable shortwave radio station for clandestine, or emergency-rescue, use by aircrews downed in remote enemy territory, operating in the frequency range 3 to 15 MHz at distances up to 3000 miles from base. The units of the Radio Station are carried in four waterproofed plastic pouches by one or more persons. Two operators are needed when the hand generator is used.

Transmitter: Frequency is controlled by plug-in crystals in two bands, covering: (1) 3 to 7 MHz and (2) 7 to 16.5 MHz with RF output of 6 to 10 watts depending on frequency, using open wire antennas of random length, preferably one-quarter wave long. The case is 6¾" × 5" × 2³⁄₃₂"; weight 2 lb 14 oz.

Receiver: eight-tube superheterodyne with two bands receiving AM or CW, 3 to 6.5 and 6.5 to 15 MHz, with continuous tuning or fixed-frequency by plug-in crystal. The case is 6¾" × 5" × 2¼"; weight 3 lb 2 oz.

Power Supply: operates from AC mains 70 to 270 V or from a 6-V accumulator and delivers 400-V DC, and 6-V heater supplies to the Filter Unit; and also provides for recharging a 6-V battery from AC mains. Size 8¹⁄₁₆" × 4" × 2³⁄₁₆"; weight 5 lb 11 oz

Filter Box, RA-6: contains smoothing circuits and two 90-V regulator tubes to give smooth, stable HT to the receiver, serving as a junction box for the RT-6 and RR-6, and stores ear-set, cords, and cables; also used when a Hand-Cranked Generator, Type GN-58, is used in place of the RP-6 when mains and 6-V storage battery are unavailable.

Accessory Pouch: carries 100 ft of antenna wire, antenna insulators, battery clamps, and inter-unit cable, plus a spare lamp bulb.

Weight . . . . . . the complete station, less 6-V battery and
                        GN-58 generator, approx. 21 lb
Official name . . . . Radio Station, Portable; Type RS-6
Circa 1953

RADIO STATION; RS-8

DESCRIPTION: A complete shortwave radio station with facilities for sending high-speed CW (Morse) signals, and reception of CW and AM in the range 2 to 20 MHz. Miniature components and transistors are used, with manual or automatic keying, and with capability for burst transmissions.

The modules and accessories of the station are fitted into a small portable case and comprise:

Transceiver: (combined transmitter receiver) 2–20 MHz in 4 bands

Power Supply Unit: operating from AC mains 90 to 240 V or from 10 to 17 V DC (an automobile supply or 12-V battery)

Antenna Base: with matching for whip antenna, the sections of which are stored in the lid of the case, together with a Ground Spike

Tape-Making Device: (coder) Type CO-8B

Tape Keyer: (for transmitting) Type KO-8B

Tape Player: with interchangeable cassettes

Storage: for tape cassettes, headphones, manual Morse key, cables and sundry spares, transmitting units and crystals

Receiver: a superheterodyne with an RF stage, which may be continuously tuned or set to fixed (spot) frequencies by a plug-in crystal. The receiver has a high-selectivity crystal filter in the 1.75 MHz IF amplifier. A BFO provides for CW (Morse) reception.

Transmitter: RF output of 3 watts, it can be keyed manually in normal way, or via a knob on the Tape Player to "IDY" (Identify), or at high speed via the Tape Keyer, using a prerecorded tape made on the Tape-Making Device CO-8B. The transmitter frequency is crystal-controlled only.

Weight . . . . 23 lb
Official name   . . . . Radio Station, Portable; Type RS-8
Circa 1966

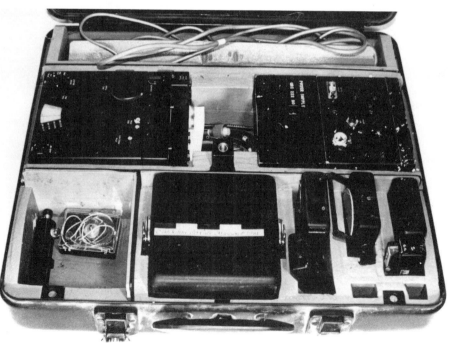

SHORTWAVE RECEIVER; RR/D-11

DESCRIPTION: The RR/D-11 is an all-transistor, dual-conversion superheterodyne receiver solidly built in a die-cast metal case with neoprene rubber seals to protect against moisture. All controls and connectors are recessed for protection.

PURPOSE: The design and construction of the RR/D-11 affords communication-receiver performance, with high stability in rugged conditions, and easy operation. Its small size and powerful performance will enable personnel operating in unfriendly areas to reliably receive both CW and voice communications.

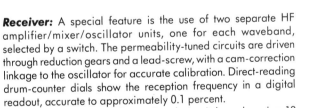

Receiver: A special feature is the use of two separate HF amplifier/mixer/oscillator units, one for each waveband, selected by a switch. The permeability-tuned circuits are driven through reduction gears and a lead-screw, with a cam-correction linkage to the oscillator for accurate calibration. Direct-reading drum-counter dials show the reception frequency in a digital readout, accurate to approximately 0.1 percent.

The circuits are on four printed-circuit boards, using 13 transistors and miniature components. The first IF is 1.55 MHz; the second IF amplifier (455 kHz) includes a mechanical bandpass filter to give high selectivity. A beat-frequency oscillator can be switched on and varied in pitch for CW (Morse) reception.

Note: The receiver is not serviceable in the field, but must be replaced and returned to base workshops for repair.

Power supply . . .	operated from external 6- or 12-V batteries or a mains-powered supply via a nine-pin connector
Output	provision is made for an external audio amplifier and loudspeaker, which may be incorporated in the power supply
Phones	phono and jack sockets provide for headphones and/or tape recorder.

Frequency range 3 to 30 MHz in two bands, 3-12 and 12-30
Reception modes . . . . AM, CW
Sensitivity . . . . ca. 5 microvolts CW, 15 microvolts AM
Selectivity . . . . . ca. 5 kHz, dB bandwidth: 16 kHz at 60 dB
Power supply . . . . . . 6- or 12-V DC external battery or PSU
Dimensions . . . . 8¾″ × 5¼″ × 1⅝″
Weight . . . . 4¼ lb
Official name . . . . Radio Receiver, Portable; RR/D-11
Circa 1959

MINIATURE RADIO STATION

DESCRIPTION: A set of 13 small modules which may be assembled by the user into different configurations. The modules plug together in a folding frame to hold a chosen set of components. The resulting assembly provides a sturdy, minimum-size radio for clandestine communication.

The system comprises:

Receiver Modules: two, 4″ × 3″ × 1″, with choice of either 3–8 or 8–16 MHz range with 4 channels, selected by plug-in miniature crystals. The superheterodyne circuit uses 7 transistors and has high selectivity, set by a solid-state filter at 455 kHz IF, 2 kHz wide at 3 dB and 20 kHz at 60 dB.

A variable-frequency BFO caters for small errors in sending and receiving crystals and temperature drift. Sockets for two sets of headphones allow use of one headset and a separate tape recorder. The only controls are:

a) gain (volume) combined with on/off switch;
b) BFO frequency (+/− 3 kHz) with on/off switch; and
c) channel switch: 1–2–3–4 for the 3–8 MHz unit and 5–6–7–8 for the 8–16 MHz unit.

The receiver can be used independently since it works from two 1.5-V cells in the battery compartment, and has an AUX socket for an antenna when used away from the station.

Transmitter Modules: two, 4″ × 3″ × 1″, low power (2 to 3 watts) for either the 3–8 or 8–16 MHz bands, with 4 channels set by plug-in crystals and selected by a panel switch.

The internal tuned circuits are trimmed when the crystals are installed. A tiny Morse key is built in, using a microswitch operated by a pullout lever.

Power-Amplifier Modules: two, 4″ × 3″ × 1⅜″, for either 3–8 or 8–16 MHz bands, when plugged into the corresponding transmitter, raise the antenna power to 20 watts.

The only control is the panel switch, selecting 4 channels, numbered 1–2–3–4 for the 3–8 MHz unit and 5–6–7–8 for the 8–16 MHz unit.

PURPOSE: The Miniature Radio Station allows the user to select and configure a small, but powerful, radio station for clandestine communication. The 3–8 MHz band unit is useful for communications to 400/500 miles. The 8–16 MHz bands can make global contacts at optimum times of day and on certain frequencies.

Scale = 1 inch

Antenna Matching Networks: two, for either 3–8 or 8–16 MHz, work with either the transmitter in the low-power or with the power amplifier in the high-power assembly.

Antenna current and best matching are indicated by a panel lamp which is fed from a transistor with a switch giving 3 steps of sensitivity, thus catering for a wide range of antennas. An Off position conserves power. Two DC–DC converter modules, for low and high power, each for 6- or 12-V use. Each has a fuse and on/off switch and acts as a base for the Rx/Tx/Matching modules. The low-power unit measures 4″ × 3″ × 1⅝″. The high-power unit measures 4″ × 4⅜″ × 2″.

Dry-battery Adapter Box: one for use with the low-power assembly only; acts as a base and has an on/off switch. It contains a length of twin cable with lugs for a dry battery for the transmitter (the receivers have their own 3-V battery built in). The bottom plate hinges open for access and is secured by a large-headed screw. Size 4″ × 3″ × 1″.

Two sizes of canvas carrying bag, with center zip closure, are provided for low- and high-power assemblies and have pockets for headphones, antenna wire, etc. The headphones are flat, round, 2″ diameter × ⅜″ thick, with head strap and elastic chin band and cable with small two-pin plug; the impedance is 600 ohms.

Low-power station	In canvas bag measures 7″ × 5″ × 6½″, and weighs less than 7 lb.
High-power station	in canvas bag measures 8″ × 5″ × 6½″, and weighs less than 10 lb, depending upon selection of power supply and accessories.
Official name	Radio Station, Modular; Solid State
Circa	1968

DESCRIPTION: The Attaché Case Radio Station combines the modules of the RS-6 in a Halliburton attaché case. The result is a small, unobtrusive, unit operating in the shortwave band from 4.5 to 22 MHz on CW. It can operate at ranges up to 300 miles indoors, and to 3000 miles using an efficient outdoor antenna system. The rugged construction of the Halliburton case offers protection against damage while travelling by airline and automobile.

Transmitter: Frequency is controlled by plug-in crystals in two bands, covering: (1) 4.5 to 10 MHz and (2) 10 to 22 MHz with RF output of 6–10 watts depending on frequency-matching open wire antennas of random length, preferably one-quarter wave long.

An "earth" connection to a cold-water pipe can be used indoors, but a counterpoise wire is recommended for outdoor use, preferably as long as the antenna wire. A Morse key is mounted on the panel, with break-in operation effective in the SEND position of the Send/Receive switch. Provision is made for an external auto-keyer.

Receiver: An eight-tube superheterodyne with two bands receiving AM or CW, 4.5 to 10 and 10 to 22 MHz, with continuous tuning on a direct-reading dial. A push-button switch on a 500-kHz crystal marker generator and a vernier CAL control enable correction of the dial so that a high accuracy of frequency setting is obtained. Small earplug-type phones are supplied, and a tape recorder can be plugged into the phone sockets.

Power Supply: Operates from AC mains 90–250 V, and a combined on/off and voltage selector switch with a panel meter enables correct settings to be made. A small 6-V hand lamp accessory on a flex can be plugged into a panel socket to give light for operation or reading. A cable in the accessory compartment connecting the transmitter/receiver to the power unit is long enough to reach and plug into an external vibrator pack for operation from a 6-V storage battery.

Dimensions . . . . 18″ × 13″ × 4½″
Weight . . . . 21 lb
Official name . . . . . Radio Station, Portable; Attaché Case
Circa 1961

SURVEILLANCE RECEIVER; SRR-4

DESCRIPTION: The Surveillance Receiver SRR-4 is compact, lightweight equipment that may be used in either portable, mobile, or fixed-station installations. It is completely self-contained, except for audio monitoring equipment, and operates from an internal battery or from external power sources, both AC (110/220 V, 60 cps) and DC (minus 12 V). Two outputs permit simultaneous application of the audio output to a headset and to recording equipment.

PURPOSE: The Surveillance Receiver SRR-4 is designed for the reception of amplitude-modulated (AM), frequency-modulated (FM), continuous wave (CW) signals in the frequency range from 50 megacycles (mc) to 200 mc, and is primarily intended for general communication and surveillance monitoring applications. It can be used for monitoring from a mobile location such as an automobile, or at a fixed listening post.

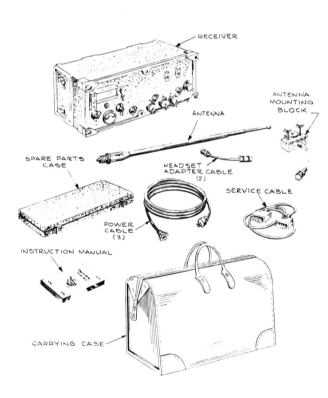

Receiver Specifications:

Type . . . . superheterodyne
Frequency ranges . . . 50 mc to 200 mc, continuously tunable
Types of reception . . . . AM, FM, CW, and MCW
Dial accuracy . . . . 0.15% (nominal)

Size . . . . 5½" × 14" × 6"
Accessories . . . . included in case
Weight . . . . 7½ lb with one battery installed
Official name . . . . . . Radio Station, Surveillance, Portable;
Model SRR-4

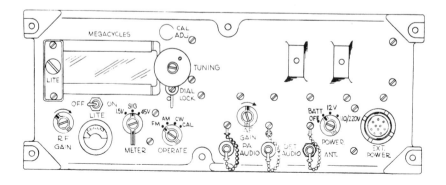

DESCRIPTION: The Delco 5300 is a transceiver operating in the frequency range of 3 to 8 megacycles (mc). The radio set is contained in a waterproof case (to a depth of three feet) and can be buried for long periods of time prior to use.

PURPOSE: The Delco 5300 is a small, lightweight portable transceiver for use by special operational personnel. It features rugged construction and the option of transmission in either voice or CW. One of the earpieces can be used as a microphone in an emergency. The "whisper switch" setting increases microphone gain to accept voice input at a reduced level.

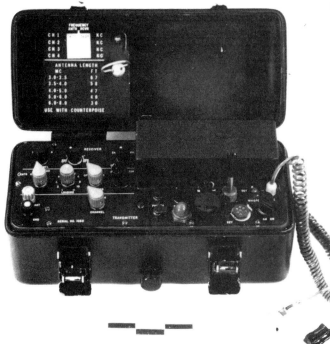

Transmitter Specifications:

Power output . . . . 5 watts CW or 1.5 watts voice
Modulation . . . . amplitude (AM)—up to 100%
Microphone . . . . 1900 ohms, magnetic
Keying speeds . . . . up to 300 wpm; will accept high-speed burst keyer
Key . . . . built in on panel or use external key
Frequency range . . . . four channels, 3 to 8 mc

Receiver Specifications:

Sensitivity . . . . 5 microvolts AM or 2 microvolts CW for 1 milliwatt output
Maximum power output . . . . 5 milliwatts
Selectivity . . . . 6 KC at 6 dB, 12 KC at 60 dB
Frequency ranges . . . . same as transmitter
Crystal type CR-78

Size . . . . 10" × 5" × 4½", plus fasteners
Battery power . . . . nickel-cadmium, rechargeable; voltage taps, 4–12–48 V
Accessories . . . . included in lid
Weight . . . . 7½ lb with one battery installed
Official name . . . Radio Station, Portable; Type Delco 5300

ONE-TIME PADS

DESCRIPTION: The One-Time Pad is a printed pad of random numbers, usually arranged in five-digit groupings. The random numbers on each page differ from the random numbers or every other page. The size of the pad is determined by the method in which it will be transported and concealed.

A One-Time Pad measuring 2" × ¾".

PURPOSE: The One-Time Pad is used to encipher and decipher messages that are absolutely unbreakable. There are two steps involved in using the pad:

a) the letters of the plain text message are converted into numbers; and

b) these numbers are added to the numbers from the One-Time Pad using noncarrying math.

Since the numbers are absolutely random, each must be used only once and thrown away to make the message unbreakable.

Many ciphers use mathematical keys that can be generated from an algorithm memorized by the agent. The resulting keys produced from the algorithm are not random, and can be broken using modern computers. The weakness of the One-Time Pad system is that replacement pads must be conveyed to the agent as the old keys are used. For that reason, One-Time Pads are usually very small.

ACTUAL SIZE

A single leaf from a One-Time Pad designed to be concealed behind a postage stamp and mailed to the agent; ⁸⁄₁₀" × ⅓".

HOW TO USE A ONE-TIME PAD

Each letter of the alphabet is assigned a numerical equivalent:

A	B	C	D	E	F	G	H	I	J	K	L	M	N	O	P	Q	R	S
01	02	03	04	05	06	07	08	09	10	11	12	13	14	15	16	17	18	19

T	U	V	W	X	Y	Z
20	21	22	23	24	25	26

Substitute the numbers for the letters in a plain text message:

S	E	R	V	I	C	E		D	E	A	D		D	R	O	P
19	5	18	22	9	3	5		4	5	1	4		4	18	15	16

Use the random numbers shown on the pad in the illustration.

Separate the One-Time Pad numbers into pairs and write them across the page (for this example we have begun with the last row of numbers on the pad). To these we add the numbers from the message.

***(Note:* When adding, use noncarrying arithmetic.)**

S	E	R	V	I	C	E	D	E	A	D	D	R	O	P
19	05	18	22	09	03	05	04	05	01	04	04	18	15	16
72	42	57	14	25	36	18	99	25	84	09	53	17	78	96
81	**47**	**65**	**36**	**24**	**39**	**13**	**93**	**20**	**85**	**03**	**57**	**25**	**83**	**02**

The message is then arranged into five-number groups and transmitted.

81476   53624   39139   32085   03572   58302

To decipher, the receiving agent, who has previously been given an identical One-Time Pad, separates the numbers into pairs, and subtracts the same set of random numbers used for encipherment:

81	**47**	**65**	**36**	**24**	**39**	**13**	**93**	**20**	**85**	**03**	**57**	**25**	**83**	**02**
72	42	57	14	25	36	18	99	25	84	09	53	17	78	96
19	05	18	22	09	03	05	04	05	01	04	04	18	15	16

These numbers are reconverted into our original message:

19	05	18	22	09	03	05	04	05	01	04	04	18	15	16
S	E	R	V	I	C	E	D	E	A	D	D	R	O	P

Official name . . . Cipher Pad, One Time; (special sizes and concealments must be specified)

Circa 1948

BURST TRANSMISSION DEVICE

DESCRIPTION: The Burst Transmission Device, AN/GRA-71, is composed of:

a) semiautomatic tape coder, MX-4496/GRA-71;
b) manual tape coder, MX-4495/GRA-71;
c) keyer adapter, MX-4498/GRA-71;
d) keyer, MX-468/GRA-71; and
e) recording tape, MA-9/GRA-71.

All components are packed within a padded, heavy-duty, moisture-proof black metal case (KA-3).

PURPOSE: The Burst Transmission Device, AN/GRA-71, is composed of an electromechanical Morse-code generator that enables an operator to record messages (in Morse-code characters) on magnetic recording tape. It has a keyer device to convert the tape-recorded Morse-code characters into equivalent electrical impulses for "keying" an associated transmitter; and a keyer adapter device that contains the electrical circuitry for supplying power to the keyer unit and adapting its output to the transmitter.

AAKRON RULE

In use, this device allows an operator to electronically enter and "compress" a coded message and "burst" it out over the transmitter in a fraction of the time required using manual Morse code. Reducing the length of time of the transmission makes it more difficult for enemy monitoring stations to record the message or pinpoint the location of the transmitter.

Deployment . . . . . . for use with radio sets: AN/GRC-109, AN/PRC-64 (Delco 5300), RS-8, etc.
Type of service . . . none (keys transmitter for CW, FSK, NSK)
Frequency range . . . . none (depends on radio set)
Power input . . . spring-motor-drive keyer, KY-468, and 6.3-V AC from transmitter to MX-4498
Power output . . . . . Electrical signals for keying transmitter for 300 wpm
Case width . . . . 9"
Case height . . . . 5¼"
Case depth . . . . 6"
Weight . . . . 9½ lb
NSN 5820-00-056-6856
REF . . . . TM 11-5835-224-12

MINIFON ATTACHÉ KIT

DESCRIPTION: The Minifon Attaché Kit is a small, portable, tape recorder and accessories contained in a leather carrying case. The kit is comprised of the following items:

    a) Minifon attaché recorder (reel-to-reel); No. 178A;
    b) wristwatch microphone; No. 105;
    c) telephone pickup; No. 111;
    d) tie-clip microphone; No. 119;
    e) dynamic microphone (tropicalized); No. 307;
    f) dual head phones; No. 101;
    g) shoulder holster; No. 517;
    h) stationary microphone; No. 329;
    i) portable speaker and power supply; No. 104;
    j) spare ¼" cassette cartridges; No. 030/128.

Minifin Recorder.

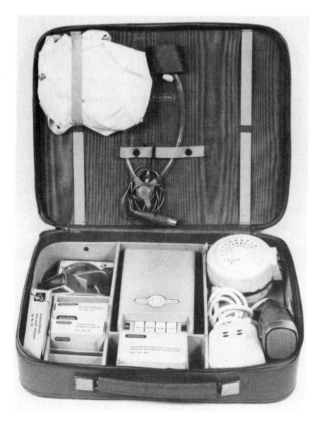

PURPOSE: The Minifon Attaché Kit combines the quality of a modern reel-to-reel tape recorder with the small size and variety of accessories required for clandestine recordings.

Recorder size . . . .   6¹¹⁄₁₆" × 3¹⁵⁄₁₆" × 1⁹⁄₁₆"
Recorder weight . . . .   1 lb 12 oz
Recorder power . . . . .   12-V dry cell battery; No. B1578; car battery; rechargeable accumulator; or AC current
Recording period . . . .   30 minutes (2 by 15 min. dual track); 60 minutes (2 by 30 min. dual track)
Attaché kit size . . . .   14½" × 3½" × 11"
Official name . . . .   Recorder, Minifon; Attaché Kit
Circa   1958

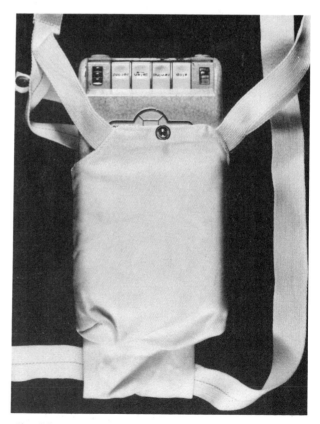

Shoulder Holster.

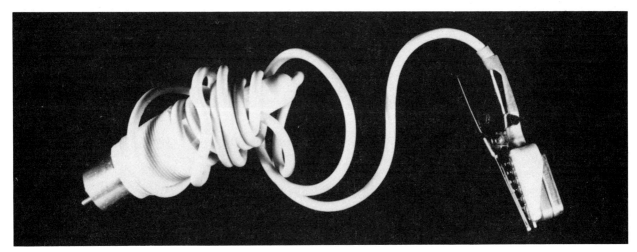

ACTUAL SIZE

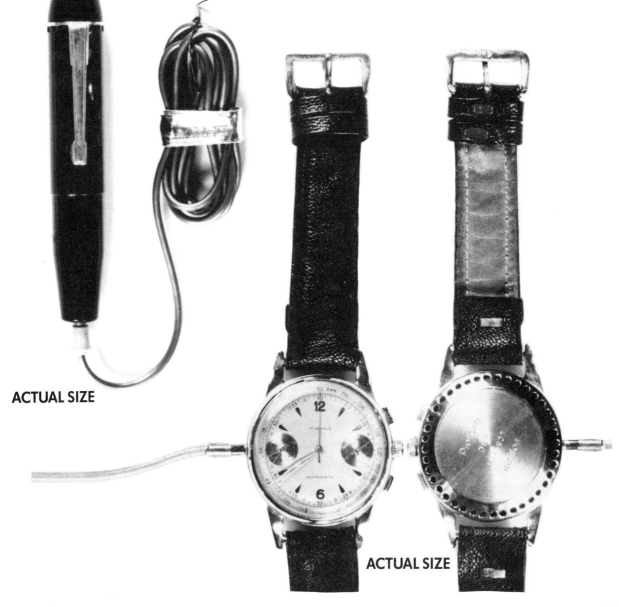

ACTUAL SIZE

ACTUAL SIZE

INFRARED COMMUNICATIONS DEVICE

DESCRIPTION: The Infrared Communications Device, LiG3, is a complete infrared transmitter and receiver unit. It contains an internal sighting scope, battery power supply, and a conventional telephone headset for voice communications.

PURPOSE: The Infrared Communications Device, LiG3, transmits and receives voice communications over distances up to three kilometers on an "invisible" beam of infrared light. Successful communication requires an unobstructed view from the two points in contact. IR communication may be successfully carried by day or night; however, its performance will be reduced dramatically by fog and heavy rain.

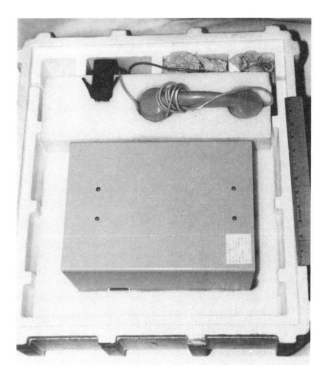

Transmitter Specifications:

Type . . . . infrared
Bandwidth . . . . 300–4000 Hz, +/−6 dB
Lamp . . . . one 2.5-V, .2 A Fa. Osram No. 3643

Receiver Specifications:

Type . . . . infrared
Bandwidth . . . . 300–3000 Hz, +/−3 dB
Photo diode . . . . one APY 10/11

The LiG3 units are intended for secure agent voice communications. This infrared (IR) communication link offers security from:

Detection: The low power radiated by the unit makes it extremely difficult to detect.
Interception: To intercept the communication a monitoring unit would have to physically disrupt the light beam. Disrupting the beam signals both parties and stops transmission.
Jamming: Jamming would have to be done optically, and would require overpowering the communication light beam in the direct line of sight. Such tactics are highly unlikely, and would be detectable by the users.

For communication, two units, LiG3, are required.

Size . . . . 320 mm × 265 mm × 140 mm
Weight . . . . 6 Kg
Temperature range . . . . −10° C to +45° C
Accessories . . . . included in case
Official name . . . . Communications Device, Infrared;
Model LiG3
Circa 1970

BRIEFCASE RECORDER

DESCRIPTION: The dark brown Briefcase Recorder contains a Uher Model 4000-L reel-to-reel tape recorder. The case has been modified with the addition of a concealed On switch on the right side of the unit, and a concealed Off switch on the left side of the unit. The sensitive microphone is mounted inside the latch bracket. The case shows no external signs of modification.

PURPOSE: The Briefcase Recorder is designed to serve as a memory aid, as well as to obtain clandestine recordings of normal conversations within a range from eight to ten feet of the concealed microphone. The concealed switches, beneath the leather, on each side of the case permit remote operation (on/off) of the Uher 4000-L without the need to open the case. The recorder has four possible speed selections:

$^{15}/_{16}$ ips: 8 hours total (2 × 4 hours per side)
$1^{7}/_{8}$ ips: 4 hours total (2 × 2 hours per side)
$3^{3}/_{4}$ ips: 2 hours total (2 × 1 hour per side)
$7^{1}/_{2}$ ips: 1 hour total (2 × ½ hour per side)

Slower tape speeds produce longer recording times, but also have a lower sound quality.

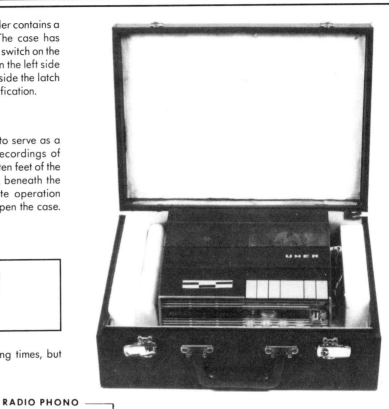

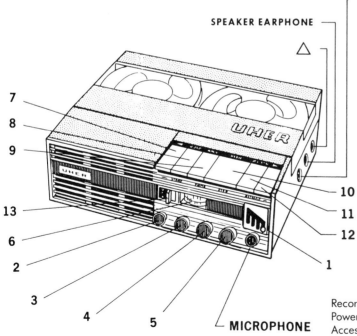

RADIO PHONO

SPEAKER EARPHONE

MICROPHONE

1-Speed Selector
2-Volume Control
3-Tone Control
4-Record Level Control
5-Automatic Level Control Selector
6-Record Signal Level/Battery Condition Meter
7-Rewind Key
8-Start/Power Key
9-Pause Control Key
10-Stop Key
11-Recording Key
12-Fast Forward Key
13-Digital Counter

Recorder . . . . Uher 4000-L; reel-to-reel
Power . . . . 5 "C" flashlight cells
Accessories . . . . dual headphones
. . . . handheld microphone
. . . . nickel-cadmium battery No. Z214
. . . . AC power adapter/charger
Size . . . . 16½" × 12" × 5¾"
Weight . . . . 16½ lb
Official name . . . . Recorder, Tape; Portable: Briefcase
Circa 1970

HOMING BEACON

DESCRIPTION: The Homing Beacon is a small, electronic device that transmits a continuous signal on a preset frequency. The beacon shown here is concealed beneath the lining in the lid of an ordinary portable typewriter. This particular device is powered by sixty (60) flat "poker chip" batteries wired in parallel for an extended transmission life.

PURPOSE: The Homing Beacon transmits a signal that can be received on standard monitoring radios. By triangulation from multiple receivers, the location of the Beacon can be determined. The Beacon may be monitored from airborne units as well as ground receivers. While the Beacon shown here has been concealed within a standard typewriter case, other concealments may be selected for specific applications.

Circuitry . . . . transistorized
Power . . . . 3 V
Range . . . . ground to air: up to five miles
. . . . . . ground to ground: 100 yards to one-half mile
depending on terrain and obstructions

Weight . . . . . . dependent on numbers of batteries utilized
Concealments . . . . available in briefcases, luggage, furniture, rifle stocks, etc.
Official name . . . . Transmitter, Beacon; Concealment Case
Circa 1966

BODY MICROPHONES

DESCRIPTION: The Body Microphones are ordinary wardrobe accessories that have been modified by the addition of miniature concealed microphones. For better audio pickup, each item has been altered slightly to create a tiny air hole in the face of the device.

PURPOSE: The Body Microphones are intended to pick up conversations in the immediate vicinity of the wearer. The resulting audio signal can be recorded using a small tape recorder concealed on the wearer, or connected to a body transmitter and sent to a nearby monitoring receiver.

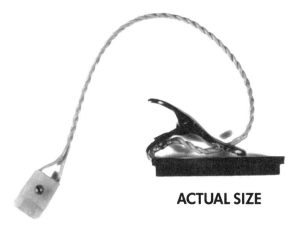

ACTUAL SIZE

Examples of Body Microphones include:

a) tie clip: ebony front with pinhole-size air hole; and
b) man's belt buckle with a small pinhole added (adjacent to the beard on the bust).

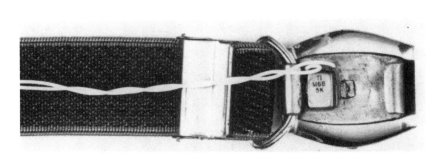

ACTUAL SIZE

Official names . . . . . . Microphone, Concealed; Belt Buckle
. . . . Microphone, Concealed; Tie Clip
Circa 1965

SILENT HAMMER

DESCRIPTION: The Silent Hammer is a small aluminum tool with a flat, rounded "mushroom" handle. At the other end of the tool is a hollow tip and rubber O-ring to hold a nail inside.

PURPOSE: The Silent Hammer is intended for use during the clandestine installation of audio or visual surveillance equipment requiring silence. With this tool, nails and tacks can be "forced" or "pushed" instead of being hammered. The nail is driven into the wall, or other surface, by an internal piston connected to the handle.

Length (closed) . . . . 6¼"
Handle width . . . . 1⅝"
Maximum nail size . . . . ³⁄₁₆" head diameter
Power . . . . manual
Weight . . . . 8 oz
Official name . . . . Tool, Hammer; Suppressed

ACTUAL SIZE

DESCRIPTION: The SK-8A Intelligence Case is contained within a standard "Royal Traveller" executive briefcase, in moulded hard plastic on an aluminum frame. The case includes a reel-to-reel tape recorder, units of a radio link, and various accessories for audio intelligence gathering.

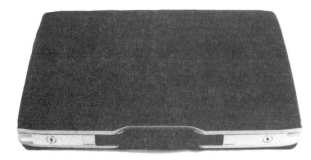

PURPOSE: The SK-8A Intelligence Case is a self-contained kit for audio intelligence gathering. Its components can be combined in a number of unique ways.

Radio Link: comprises two cigarette-pack-size metal cases, a Receiver and a Transmitter, operating from internal batteries in the VHF radio band and having a range of a few blocks in town or several miles in open country.

Tape Recorder: battery-operated, low-speed reel-to-reel machine giving up to six hours' recording. It can be operated manually, or in unattended stand-by mode (to be started automatically on receipt of a signal via the radio link), stopping when the signal stops, thus conserving tape and batteries. A local microphone can insert comments on the tape for operational notations.

The tape recorder may be operated in an automobile, using the 12-V supply from the cigar lighter socket to conserve the recorder batteries. An adapter can be used so that the radio link receiver uses the automobile antenna to extend the working range of the set. It can also work from 110-V AC mains.

The Radio Link Can Be Used:

a) person to person;
b) with transmitter hidden on location and receiver on surveilling agent;
c) with receiver in the tape recorder, a signal from the transmitter will start the recorder; or
d) an operator at the tape recorder can monitor the signal and record at will.

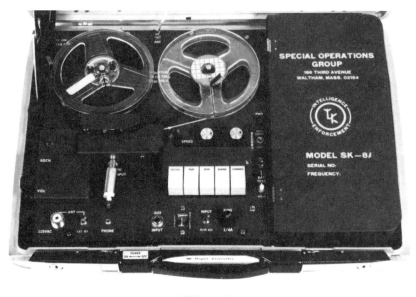

The Accessories Include:

a) miniature microphone with a 16" flex cord which also acts as a transmitting antenna;
b) small earphone with lead which acts as receiving antenna; and
c) clip-on (induction) telephone pickup with cord acting as a transmitting antenna.

Dimensions: .... 18½" × 13½" × 3½"
Weight .... 16 lb
Official name .... Intelligence Case; Model SK-8A
Circa 1973

ATTACHÉ CASE RECORDER

DESCRIPTION: The Attaché Case Recorder is a standard "GSA issue" black leather case of ordinary appearance. There is no visual indication on the exterior or interior of the case to suggest it has been modified.

The on/off switch is attached internally to the left-hand sliding latch. The recorder is turned on by sliding the latch "up," instead of the normal outward sliding movement necessary to open the case. The recorder is turned off by sliding the same switch "down."

The small Pearlcorder S801 is hidden in the top of the lid of the case behind the partition and held in place by a Velcro® strip. Two color-coded male plugs are provided for connections to the REM (remote) and MIC (microphone) sockets.

PURPOSE: The Attaché Case Recorder is capable of recording normal conversations within a 20-foot radius of the attaché case. The special Electret microphone has an internal noise suppresser and amplifier mounted inside the left-hand latch-way opening. The sound quality is consistently good with the latch either open or closed.

Contained Within the Case Are:

a) Pearlcorder S801 microcassette recorder (modified internally);
b) special Electret microphone mounted inside the left-hand latch-way opening; and
c) special on/off switch attached to the left-hand sliding latch.

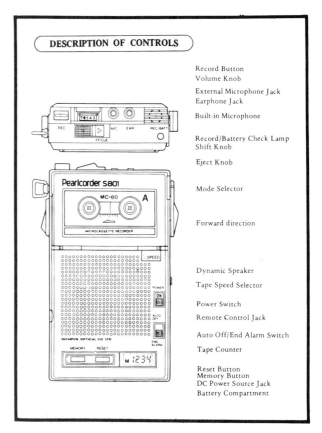

DESCRIPTION OF CONTROLS

Record Button
Volume Knob

External Microphone Jack
Earphone Jack

Built-in Microphone

Record/Battery Check Lamp
Shift Knob

Eject Knob

Mode Selector

Forward direction

Dynamic Speaker

Tape Speed Selector

Power Switch

Remote Control Jack

Auto Off/End Alarm Switch

Tape Counter

Reset Button
Memory Button
DC Power Source Jack
Battery Compartment

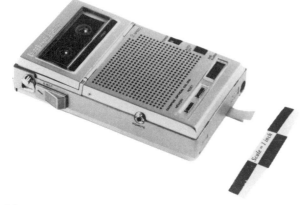

Recorder	Pearlcorder S801
Recorder size	4¼" × 2½" × ⅞"
Recording time	60 minutes per side for the MC-60 tape at 1.2 cm/sec recording speed
Power	two 1.5-V "AA" batteries
Microphone	special Electret
Attaché case size	18" × 4¾" × 13"
Accessories	adapter for recording telephone conversations
Case weight	7½ lb
Official name	Recorder, Attaché Case

DESCRIPTION: The Motel Kit is contained in a small leather travelling case. It is comprised of the following components:

a) amplifier unit, separate controls for gain and volume;
b) stethoscopic earphones;
c) two contact microphones;
d) connecting cable; and
e) spare 9-V battery.

PURPOSE: The Motel Kit contains a sensitive transducer that picks up the actual vibrations on the target wall coming from sound (conversation) in the adjacent room. The extremely sensitive contact microphone is pressed firmly against the door or wall and the resulting vibrations amplified and sent to the earphones or an optional tape recorder. For better audio, or extended operations, tape or glue the contact mike solidly to the wall.

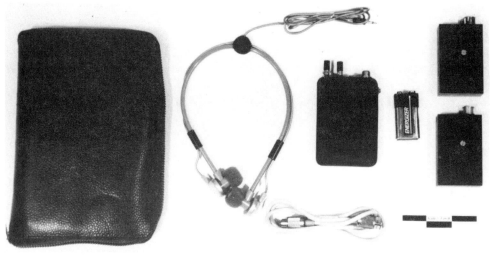

Amplifier	solid-state
Amplifier size	$4\frac{1}{4}'' \times 2\frac{1}{2}'' \times \frac{7}{8}''$
Amplifier power	one 9-V battery
Microphone	two contact microphones
Case size	$8\frac{1}{2}'' \times 6'' \times 1\frac{1}{2}''$
Case weight	20 oz
Official name	Amplifier, Contact; Kit

Note: For maximum effectiveness, the door or wall should be solid. Hollow doors or walls reduce the effective transmission of the sound and must be attacked with different tools to achieve an acceptable sound level.

SOUND DETECT KIT

DESCRIPTION: The Sound Detect Kit is a complete audio counter-intelligence kit contained in a leather briefcase. The kit is comprised of the following items:

a) amplifier unit, model No. SU-102B;
b) metal detector unit;
c) contact microphone;
d) general utility microphone;
e) carbon microphone;
f) test clips;
g) induction coil;
h) RF probe; and
i) recorder adapter.

PURPOSE: The Sound Detect Kit provides audio technicians with the countermeasures equipment necessary for locating illicit microphones and "soundproofing" a room. The equipment provided may also be used for limited audio "sound gathering."

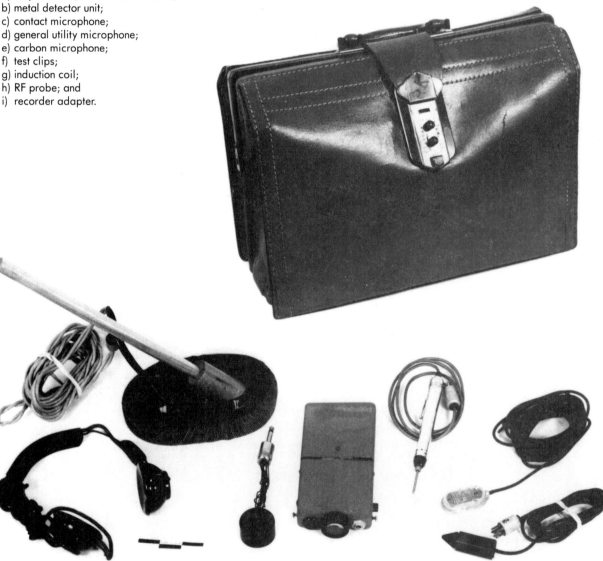

Amplifier Unit: All other attachments plug into this amplifier, and are used in conjunction with it.

Metal Detector Unit: aids security agent in locating hidden microphones "planted" in the wall or furniture.

Contact Microphone: aids the security agent to check if conversations can be picked up through the wall.

General Utility Microphone: for listening to conversations through a wall or partition.

Carbon Microphone: for use as a "plant" microphone.

Test Clips: check telephones to see if they are "safe" and to listen in on telephone conversations.

Induction Coil: picks up a two-way telephone conversation without the necessity for making any direct connections to the telephone wires or to the telephone.

RF Probe: to locate small battery-operated radio transmitters and carrier-type transmitters using the power line as a means of transmission.

Recorder Adapter: provides a means of coupling the output of the amplifier to the input of a recorder.

Kit size . . . . 16" × 12" × 7"
Power . . . . two batteries: Eveready No. 1040, 1½ V; Eveready No. 412, 22½ V

Weight . . . . 12 lb
Order as . . . . . Countermeasures Kit, Audio; Sound Detect
Circa 1964

DESCRIPTION: The Fine Wire Kit is contained in a small, portable metal case. The components are shown in the illustration.

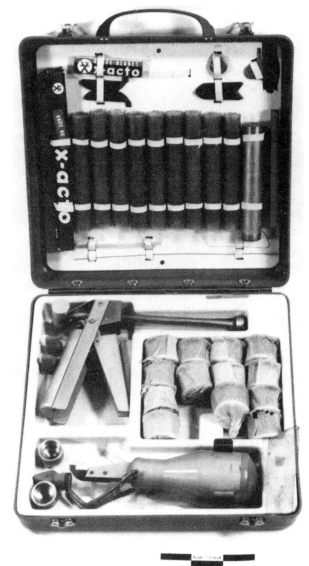

PURPOSE: The tools in the kit can be used to lay a concealed wire as part of an installation of microphones, transmitters, and other audio devices. The cable can be forced into cracks or actually embedded in soft building materials without damage to the fine wires of which the cable is composed. With this equipment it is possible to lay a fine wire across an exposed wall without any visual signs of the installation.

The wire-laying tool has an internal monitoring circuit to warn the operator should a break in the wire occur during installation.

Kit size . . . . 9" × 2⅜" × 9¾"
Power . . . . two 1.3-V nickel-cadmium; or Mallory RM 630 R
Weight . . . . 4½ lb
Official name . . . . Audio Installation Kit, Fine Wire

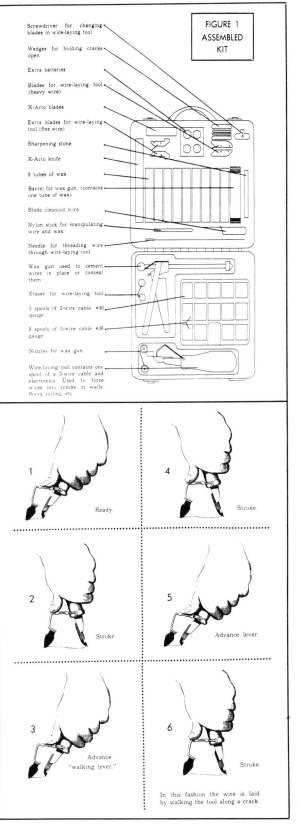

FIGURE 1
ASSEMBLED
KIT

Screwdriver for changing blades in wire-laying tool

Wedges for holding cracks open

Extra batteries

Blades for wire-laying tool (heavy wire)

X-Acto blades

Extra blades for wire-laying tool (fine wire)

Sharpening stone

X-Acto knife

9 tubes of wax

Barrel for wax gun (contains one tube of wax)

Blade cleanout wire

Nylon stick for manipulating wire and wax

Needle for threading wire through wire-laying tool

Wax gun used to cement wires in place or conceal them

Eraser for wire-laying tool

5 spools of 2-wire cable, #30 gauge

9 spools of 3-wire cable #38 gauge

Nozzles for wax gun

Wire-laying tool contains one spool of a 3-wire cable and electronics. Used to force wires into cracks in walls, floors, ceiling, etc.

1 Ready.

2 Stroke

3 Advance "walking lever."

4 Stroke.

5 Advance lever.

6 Stroke.

In this fashion the wire is laid by walking the tool along a crack.

HOT-MIKE TELEPHONES

DESCRIPTION: The three telephone desk sets shown here have not been modified externally. Internally, however, each set has been rewired so that the telephone's carbon mouthpiece may be activated, even while the handset is in the "hung up" position.

These sets have been internally modified by "hot miking" for operational use:

PURPOSE: The process of shorting, or bypassing, the set's hook switch in a manner that does not affect the normal operation of the telephone, but causes the unused telephone to become a microphone, is called "hot miking." The objective of these changes is to permit the telephone's carbon mouthpiece to be activated by allowing a small, nearly undetectable amount of direct current to flow through the instrument.

Once the room audio is passed through the unused instrument onto the outgoing lines, the eavesdropper may intercept it only at a point between the modified instrument and the first telephone company switching exchange. A listening post (LP) must be established to record the resulting audio signals at a location with access to the wires, but before the first switching exchange.

a) East German "Alpha" set; Veb Fernmeldewerk, Nordhausen; Type 551-11207. This set was used throughout East Germany and in other communist nations.

b) Oki Electric Industry Co. Ltd; Model H-224, 4-A Automatic Telephone Set. This set is commonly found in North Korea, Southeast Asia, and throughout the Pacific Rim countries.

c) Dutch desk set designed by Ericson, but manufactured by CTD in Paris; Soctel 363. This set was found throughout Vietnam and other Southeast Asian countries whose national telephone exchanges had been installed by French companies.

Size, weight, and color . . . . identical to the standard telephone handset in use in the target country

Official name . . . . . . Telephone, Modified; Special (model, color, and wiring information must be specified at time of order)

Circa 1958

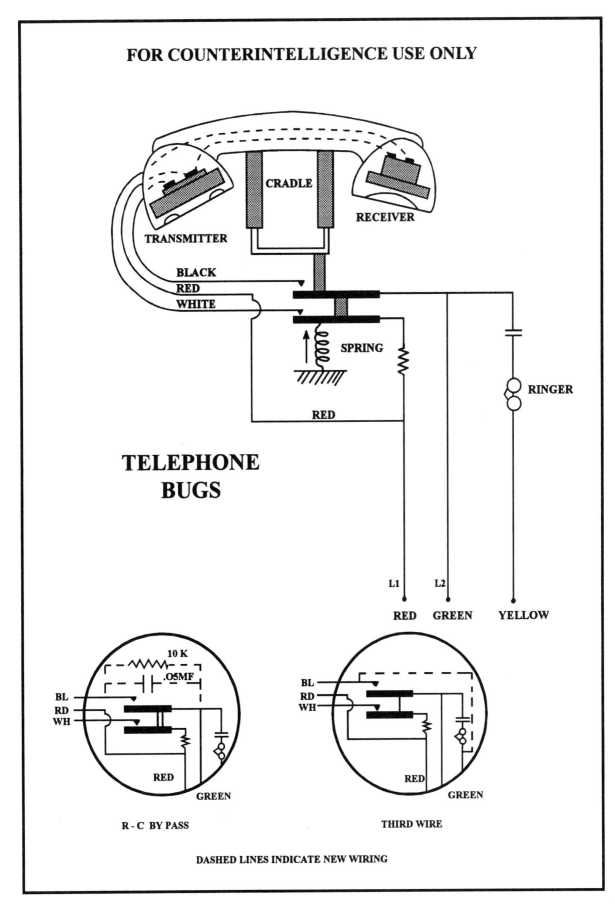

CLANDESTINE LISTENING DEVICES

DESCRIPTION: The Clandestine Listening Devices, or "Bugs" shown here, are identical externally to common items to be found at home or in the office. Each piece has been modified internally with the addition of a miniaturized clandestine microphone and transmitter.

PURPOSE: The Clandestine Listening Devices are camouflaged as common electrical items that might be found in the home or office. These devices are powered by the line current passing through them, so they may operate for indefinite periods of time without the necessity of battery replacement. Each item is capable of picking up normal conversation within a 15-foot range, and transmitting it to a monitoring receiver and tape recorder set up in a nearby listening post (LP).

Examples of Modified Electrical Items Include:

a) standard 110-V appliance plug;
b) standard three-way plug, 110-V;
c) European 220-V three-way extension plug; and
d) standard "C" cell flashlight battery.

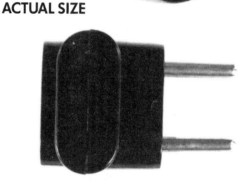

ACTUAL SIZE

Official name . . . . Transmitter, Concealed; Special;
(specify the type of device needed,
and country of intended use)
Circa 1967

1) *Inside picture frame*
2) *Inside TV set*
3) *Lamp*
4) *In table leg*
5) *In lighter*
6) *In ashtray*
7) *Hot-mike telephone*
8) *In overhead light*

"DOG DOO" TRANSMITTER

DESCRIPTION: The "Dog Doo" Transmitter is camouflaged to resemble the excrement of a medium-size dog, or other similar animal. Contained within the device is a beacon transmitter and three long-life nickel-cadmium batteries.

PURPOSE: The "Dog Doo" Transmitter is a homing beacon that sends out a signal to monitoring aircraft several miles away. The beacon can be used by an agent, or other operational personnel, to mark a specific location for aerial reconnaissance, further observation, or a possible air strike. The camouflage has been selected to reduce the probability of the unit being disturbed after being left at the target.

ACTUAL SIZE

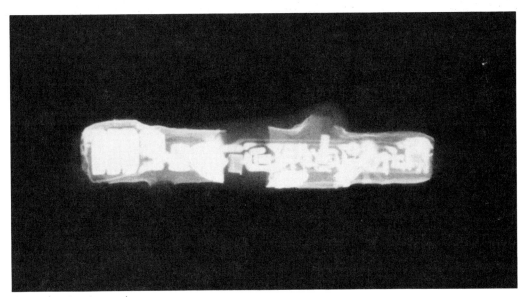

X-ray showing internal components.

Size . . . . 4¼" long, 1" diameter
Weight . . . . 4 oz

Official name . . . . Radio, Transmitter, T-1151v/USG
Straight Stitch Peat Moss
FSN 5820-437-1895
Issued by . . . . Military Intelligence
Circa 1970

LOCK-PICK KNIFE

DESCRIPTION: The Lock-Pick Knife appears to be a common pocketknife. Inside, however, are:

a) three "feeler" picks of varying radius;
b) one straight diamond-end pick;
c) one "riffle" pick;
d) one "skeleton," or lever-lock, pick; and
e) one torsion (torque) wrench.

PURPOSE: The Lock-Pick Knife is a small, portable device that provides the operator with ready access to a specially designed tool for picking both American pin-tumbler and European lever locks. The torque wrench is packed within the knife and may be accessed beneath the lever-lock pick. The "knife" can be discreetly carried in pocket or purse, and will pass unnoticed in a cursory search.

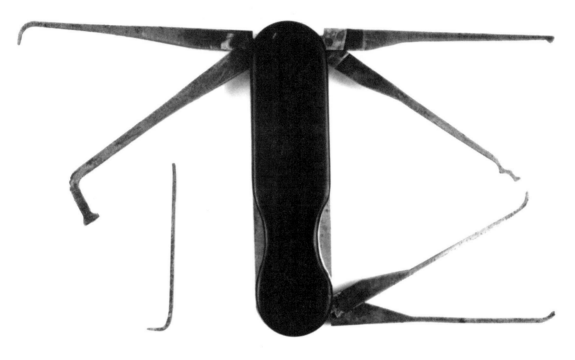

ACTUAL SIZE

Length	3¼"
Width	⅞"
Picks	2½"
Official name	Lock-Pick Set, Portable; Knife
Circa	1950

LOCK-PICK KIT

DESCRIPTION: The Lock-Pick Kit is a professional assortment of lock picks and tools packed within a small, black leather case. Inside are:

a) a general assortment of picks, including full, half, and three-quarter rakes, diamond-tip picks, single, double, and half-double ball picks;

b) light-, medium-, and heavyweight tension wrenches of various lengths and styles; and

c) hook- and saw-type broken key extractors.

PURPOSE: The Lock-Pick Kit is a small, portable case containing sixty (60) special tools designed for the efficient opening of most pin-tumbler, wafer, lever, and double-sided locks.

Note: The proper use of this kit requires special training and instruction.

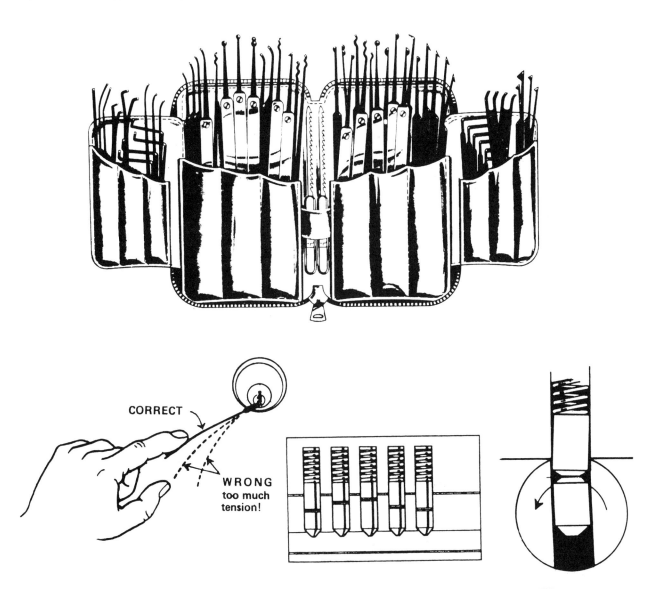

CORRECT

WRONG
too much
tension!

PINS BIND IN ORIGINAL, LOCKED POSITION WHEN TOO MUCH TENSION IS APPLIED

Height . . . . 6¾"	Official name . . . . Lock-Pick Kit, Professional;
Width . . . . 13"	Model No. NDPK-60
Weight . . . . 1 lb	

LOCK-PICK GUN

DESCRIPTION: The Lock-Pick Gun is a metal lock-picking device in the configuration of a small pistol. Both straight and offset picks are available to accommodate different locks and keyways. The "trigger" of the "gun" is spring loaded and can be squeezed rapidly. This trigger movement causes the pick to snap upward within the lock and transfers the striking force to the pins.

PURPOSE: The Lock-Pick Gun is an effective tool, when used with a torque wrench, for the opening of most pin-tumbler locks in less than a minute. The following instructions should be carefully followed:

1) Insert tension (torque) wrench into the bottom of keyway, opposite pins. Apply light pressure in the direction the lock is expected to turn.
2) Insert pick just below the bottom pins. The striking force must be equally distributed to all pins.
3) Once the gun and tension wrench are in place, squeeze the trigger of the gun rapidly.
4) If the lock does not open after five shots, release tension on the torsion wrench and increase the tension adjustment on the gun.
5) Do not attempt to pick one pin at a time. The pins must be picked concurrently.

Length . . . . 4" (without pick)
Height . . . . 4½"
Picks . . . . 2½"
Official name . . . . Lock-Pick, Gun
Circa 1960

ACTUAL SIZE

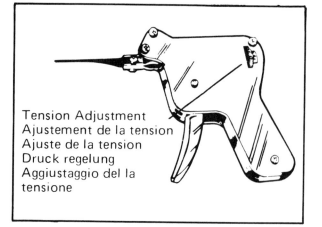

Tension Adjustment
Ajustement de la tension
Ajuste de la tension
Druck regelung
Aggiustaggio del la tensione

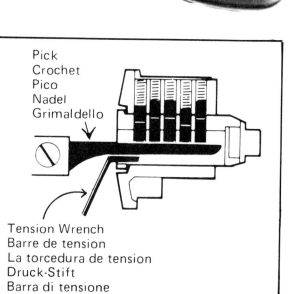

Pick
Crochet
Pico
Nadel
Grimaldello

Tension Wrench
Barre de tension
La torcedura de tension
Druck-Stift
Barra di tensione

DESCRIPTION: The Key-Impressioning Kit is a complete key-moulding kit contained in a small, olive-drab metal box. Inside the kit are the following items:

a) one two-piece aluminum mould;
b) one quantity of modelling clay;
c) one vial of talc;
d) one thimble (ladle with twisted wire handle);
e) six low-melting temperature alloy (Cerebum) slugs; and
f) candles.

Scale = 1 inch

PURPOSE: The Key-Impressioning Kit allows a duplicate metal key to be cast quickly from an original key that has been impressioned in the enclosed mould. The following steps must be taken:

1) Press the key partially into one side of the mould (allowing the bow of the key to overhang slightly).
2) Line up the other side of the mould and press together tightly.
3) Separate the halves of the mould carefully and remove the key.
4) Dust the separated moulds lightly with the talc.
5) Create a small "funnel" in the clay to facilitate the pouring of the low-melting temperature alloy into the mould.
6) Assemble the moulds together, being careful not to damage the impression. Tape or wrap the mould to ensure the halves will not separate during the casting.
7) Melt the alloy using the candles provided.
8) Carefully pour the molten alloy into the mould. Rap the mould sharply on a hard surface to ensure the equal distribution of alloy throughout the impression.
9) Keep the mould tightly closed until the metal hardens.
10) Carefully separate the two halves and lift the key straight up. The resulting new key is much weaker than the original, and should be duplicated on a key-cutting machine to produce a full-strength copy.

Dimensions . . . . 6½″ × 3¼″ × 1¼″
Official name . . . . Key-Impressioning Kit
Circa 1960

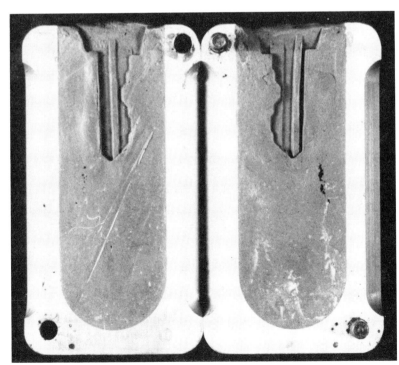

ACTUAL SIZE

Note: If operational requirements necessitate the immediate use of an impressioned key casting, it should be done with the aid of a standard torsion wrench to turn the lock cylinder.

IMPROVISED KEY-MAKING KIT

DESCRIPTION: The Improvised Key-Making Kit is issued within a small leather binder.

Contained Inside Are:

a) special impressioning tool;
b) small magnet;
c) shims—two .002″ thick;
d) "C" Clamp for holding key;
e) round pippin file;
f) flat file;
g) pin vise;
h) graphite powder;
i) emery cloth; and
j) magnifying glass.

PURPOSE: The Improvised Key-Making Kit is used by specially trained personnel to produce keys for various types of locks without the necessity of picking or disassembling the lock mechanism. It provides a fast and effective means of producing original keys to locks. It may be used with pin-tumbler mechanisms, warded, lever, and wafer locks.

As the key comes into contact with the inner parts of the locking mechanism, the pin tumblers leaves certain impressions on the top edge of key blade's surface. By successfully interpreting these marks, the agent can hand-file a key that will open the lock. In the hands of a trained specialist, many pin-tumbler locks can be opened faster, and with greater reliability, using the Improvised Key-Making Kit, than through conventional "picking" or "raking" techniques.

Case dimensions	7½″ × 5½″ × 2″
Tool length	5½″
Tool height	4¾″
Official name	Key-Making Kit, Improvised; Portable
Circa	1950

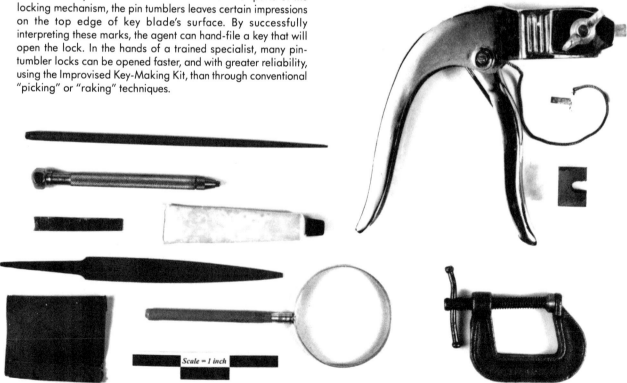

ELECTRONIC STETHOSCOPE

DESCRIPTION: The Electronic Stethoscope is issued in a small, grey plastic carrying case and consists of:

a) transistorized hi-gain amplifier;
b) contact (vibration pickup) microphone with magnet; and
c) stethoscopic earphones.

PURPOSE: The Electronic Stethoscope is designed for use during the manipulation of combination tumbler locks found on most safes manufactured prior to 1965. (After that date, major safe companies made their locks quieter to prevent this means of attack.) The magnetic contact microphone is attached adjacent to, but not touching, the dial. It picks up vibrations and transmits these to the hi-gain amplifier. The amplifier magnifies the sound of the opening cam and drop-in lever engaging in the lock 10,000 times, and sends it to the earphones. The Electronic Stethoscope is for use by properly trained personnel only.

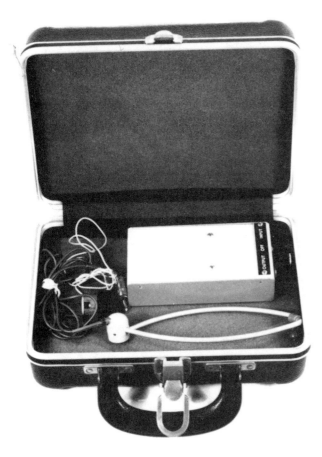

The amplifier has a combination gain control and on/off switch. The input jack is for the contact mike, and the output jack is for the earphones. The amplifier is powered by two standard 9-V alkaline batteries (Mallory No. MN-1604 recommended). Access to the battery compartment is by two large metal screw-fasteners on the bottom of the unit; turn them one-quarter turn counter-clockwise to open.

Official name . . . . Amplifier, Portable; Contact
Circa 1965

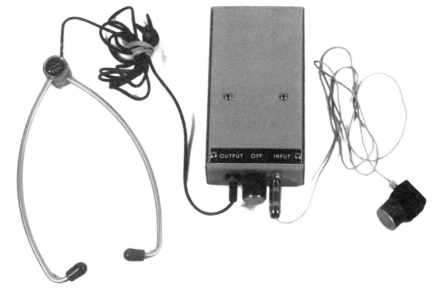

EQUIPMENT DESTROYER

DESCRIPTION: The Equipment Destroyer is a ceramic liner covered with waterproof pasteboard. The ends are sheet metal. The top is provided with a friction-type lid. The unit is packaged in foil or barrier material.

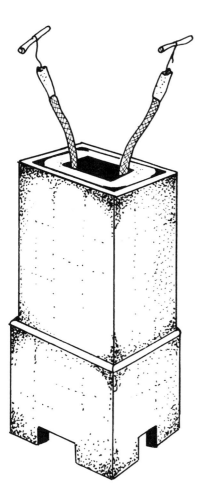

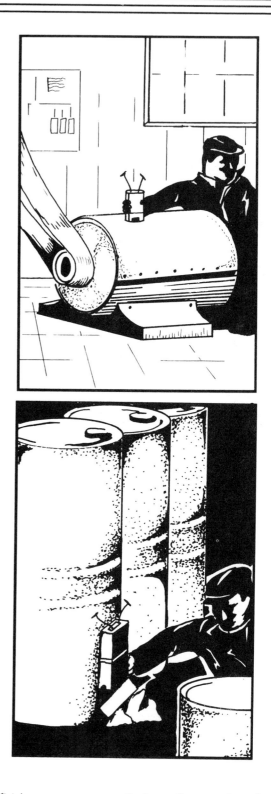

PURPOSE: The Equipment Destroyer is used to attack metallic targets, such as transformers, electric motors, gears, bearings, boilers, storage tanks, and pipelines. In operation, the device produces a quantity of molten metal that streams out of the bottom of the unit. On contact with the target the molten metal will cut through the casing and pour molten metal on some vital part. Steel casings up to three-quarter inches thick can be cut in this manner.

Weight	4 lb
Incendiary mixture	37 oz of thermite
Ignition system	dual, 20-second safety fuse with friction-type lighter
Ignition mixture	8½ grams (atomized aluminum, iron oxide, and barium peroxide)
Burning temperature	4600° F
Burning time	approximately one minute
Performance effect	will penetrate ¾″ of steel

Official name	Equipment Destroyer, Incendiary; Thermite Well (Revised)
FSN	1375-H02-1690
Circa	1949

78

DESCRIPTION: The Combustible Notebook is a leather-bound spiral loose-leaf notebook measuring four inches by six inches. The pages of paper are interleaved with Pyrofilm® in a ratio of one to three, by weight. A special incendiary pencil (no delay, instant ignition) is fitted inside the notebook. The release pin on the incendiary pencil has been camouflaged to resemble a pencil eraser.

PURPOSE: The Combustible Notebook is used for the destruction of cryptographic material, signal plans, operational notes, and other written or printed material of possible value to the enemy. When the safety pin has been removed and the eraser removed, instant ignition is provided by a release-type spring-loaded plunger and firing pin, acting upon a magnesium incendiary. Complete destruction of the material will be achieved in 30 seconds.

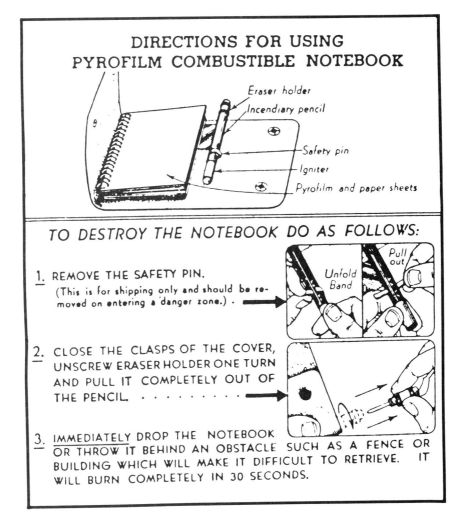

DIRECTIONS FOR USING PYROFILM COMBUSTIBLE NOTEBOOK

Eraser holder
Incendiary pencil
Safety pin
Igniter
Pyrofilm and paper sheets

TO DESTROY THE NOTEBOOK DO AS FOLLOWS:

1. REMOVE THE SAFETY PIN.
   (This is for shipping only and should be removed on entering a danger zone.)

   Pull out — Unfold Band

2. CLOSE THE CLASPS OF THE COVER, UNSCREW ERASER HOLDER ONE TURN AND PULL IT COMPLETELY OUT OF THE PENCIL.

3. IMMEDIATELY DROP THE NOTEBOOK OR THROW IT BEHIND AN OBSTACLE SUCH AS A FENCE OR BUILDING WHICH WILL MAKE IT DIFFICULT TO RETRIEVE. IT WILL BURN COMPLETELY IN 30 SECONDS.

Size . . . . 4" × 6"
Ignition system . . . . . special incendiary pencil, zero delay
Combustible material . . . . Pyrofilm
Burning time . . . . 30 seconds
Performance effect . . . . complete destruction

Official name . . . . Notebook, Incendiary
Circa 1948

DUST EXPLOSION INITIATOR

DESCRIPTION: The Dust Explosion Initiator is an aluminum tube twelve inches long and two inches in diameter. The end caps are threaded and recessed to hold shipping plugs which are removed when the device is primed. The casing is filled with 360 grams—60 percent granulated trinitrotoluene (TNT) and 40 percent powdered magnesium—of explosive.

PURPOSE: The Dust Explosion Initiator is designed for blowing up targets (such as boxcars, warehouses, ship's holds, or factory buildings) which have confined spaces and limited ventilation. The dust explosion is induced by detonating a charge of explosive mixed with incendiary material in either a container of highly volatile flammable liquid, or in a bed of flammable dust. Upon detonation a cloud of dust is dispersed in the surrounding area. When the oxygen ratio reaches the explosive range, the incendiary ignites the cloud.

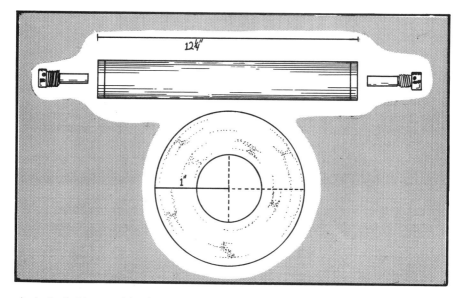

The Initiator can be ignited with an AC delay fuse with M-34 detonator, or a clockwork firing device. Once armed, the Initiator may be inserted into a 25- to 100-pound bag of flour or a two-gallon can of gasoline. When other highly combustible liquids, or easily combustible powders, are to be used with the Initiator, the specific material should first be trial-tested against a structure similar to the intended target.

Length . . . . 12"
Diameter . . . . 2"
Pack . . . . single initiator tube
Official name . . . . Charge, Demolition; Dust Explosion Initiator Type
FSN 1375-H00-0007
Circa 1953

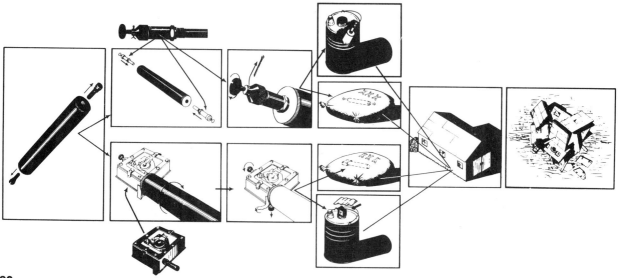

DESCRIPTION: The Firestarter is a magnesium head about two inches long and five-sixteenths of an inch in diameter containing an igniting mix and thermite. Five of the items are packed in a small tear-can and are protected from moisture by a rubber plug and a waterproof plastic sleeve.

PURPOSE: The device was designed to be used with a standard time pencil or with a time fuse (both must be obtained separately). When initiated, it burns fiercely at 4500° F for a few seconds. Due to this brief burning period, it will ignite only light materials and other incendiaries.

The Firestarter will not ignite properly if it is submerged in a liquid such as napalm or gasoline; it needs oxygen for combustion. To ignite fluids, the Firestarter should be suspended just over the surface.

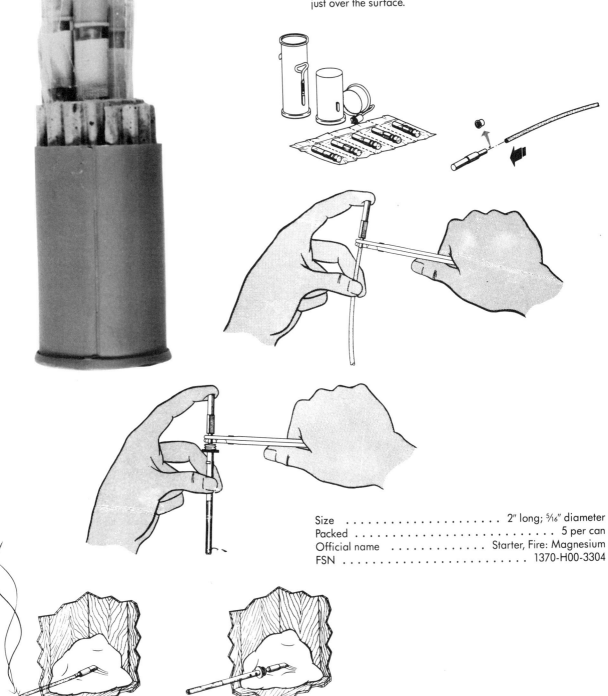

Size	2" long; 5/16" diameter
Packed	5 per can
Official name	Starter, Fire: Magnesium
FSN	1370-H00-3304

WEAPONS FIRING DEVICE

DESCRIPTION: The Weapons Firing Device consists of three parts:

   a) pull-type firing device;
   b) adapter (adjustable clamp); and
   c) spool of wire.

PURPOSE: The Weapons Firing Device can be used with an automatic weapon to create a booby-trap setup.

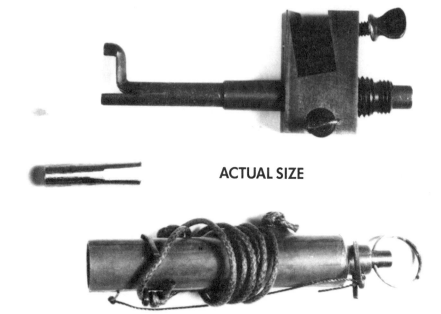

ACTUAL SIZE

Instructions
1) Screw firing device and adapter together.
2) Attach wire to pull ring.
3) a) Attach unit to weapon trigger guard.
   b) Loosen thumbscrew forward through the adapter block, carefully, until the claw engages the trigger.
   c) Tighten the thumbscrew to hold the sleeve in position.
4) Remember to keep reciprocating parts free and ejection port clear.

Operational Example
1) Fasten wire to door knob—adjust and aim weapon.
2) When gun is aimed, it can be held steady with weights or by fastening to a solid object.
3) Remove safety pins—A first, B second.
4) Weapon fires when door is opened.

Official name . . . . Firing Device, Weapons
Circa 1959

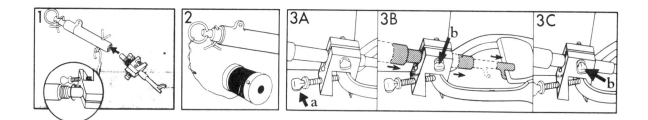

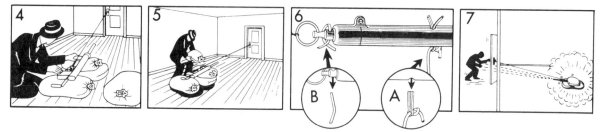

DESCRIPTION: The 24-Hour Clock is a firing device consisting of three parts:

1) clock;
2) release mechanism; and
3) firing pin.

All components have luminous numerals and pointers to permit their use at night. Safety pins are provided to prevent premature firing.

PURPOSE: The 24-Hour Clock is a precision firing device designed to trigger an explosive charge or ignite an incendiary at any elapsed time between 15 minutes and 23 hours, 45 minutes.

The hands of the clock move in a conventional clockwise direction; the hour hand, however, takes 24 hours to make one complete revolution. The numbers on the clock face are numbered counter-clockwise to show the time remaining before it fires. The clock mechanism is waterproof to a depth of 50 feet.

Using adapters, the clock can be attached to a:

1) Limpet mine;
2) Dust Initiator;
3) incendiary head of an AC delay; and
4) M-34 detonator for firing bulk charges.

Official name . . . . Firing Device, Clockwork
Stock No. 1375-H00-1931
Unit of issue . . . . single clockwork
Circa 1959

ACTUAL SIZE

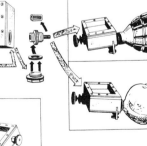

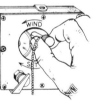

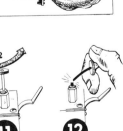

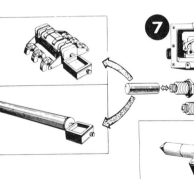

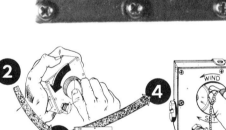

PRESSURE-RELEASE SWITCH

DESCRIPTION: The Pressure-Release Switch and its detachable-spring-snout coupling base measures 4½″ × ⅝″ × ⅝″ and weighs 3 oz. Two units, including instructions, are packed in a cardboard box.

```
Size . . . . . . . . . . . . . . . . . . . . . . . . 4½″ × ⅝″ × ⅝″
Weight  . . . . . . . . . . . . . . . . . . . . . . . . . . . . . . 3 oz
Packed . . . . . . . . . . . . . . . . . . . . . . . . single device
Official name  . . Firing Device, Demolition; Pressure Release
FSN . . . . . . . . . . . . . . . . . . . . . . . 1375-H00-0028
Circa . . . . . . . . . . . . . . . . . . . . . . . . . . . . . . 1948
```

PURPOSE: The Pressure-Release Switch is a booby-trapping item which will initiate an explosive charge when pressure bearing on the toe of the device is removed. An extension of the housing of the device, and the hinged cover, form a toe which can be inserted into the crack of a door or desk drawer or under the edge of a variety of objects (the toe is drilled to allow it to be attached to a wooden surface). Five pounds of weight or pressure on the toe will keep the cover closed and the device cocked. When the pressure is removed it will fire a primer in the coupling base, which in turn will fire a blasting cap or ignite a length of safety fuse.

ACTUAL SIZE

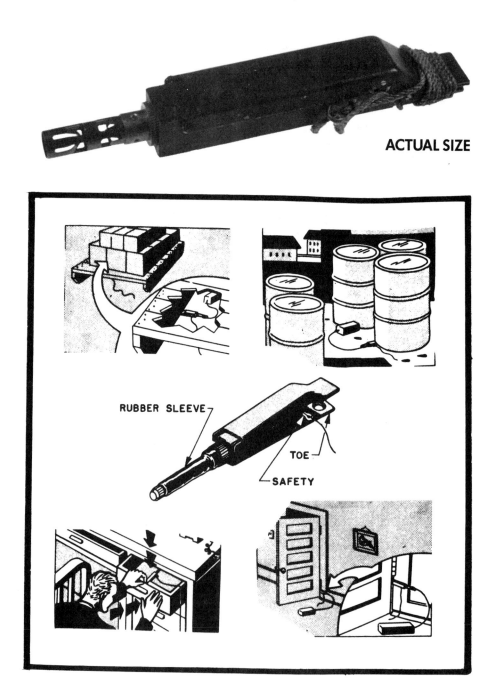

RUBBER SLEEVE

TOE

SAFETY

DESCRIPTION: The Electric Switch is about two inches long and less than one inch wide and one inch thick. Three protuberances extend the body:

a) red binding post;
b) black binding post; and
c) threaded snout containing a plunger.

PURPOSE: The Electric Switch permits the one-time closing or opening of an electric circuit by various available demolition firing devices. For long-term delays it can be used with the AC delay, or for greater accuracy, the Thirty-Day Clockwork. For shorter delays it can be coupled with a time pencil or the 24-Hour Clock; or for instantaneous booby trapping it can be coupled to the versatile pull-type firing device.

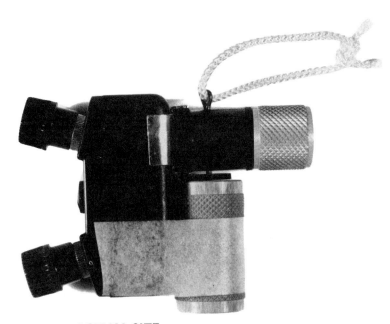

ACTUAL SIZE

The black and red binding posts are terminal connections. Between them is a screw that adjusts the switch from "normally opened" to "normally closed."

The threaded snout connector contains a plunger that opens or closes the switch when forced forward. The switch can be used with batteries, or with normal house current (115 V).

Size . . . . 2" long, 1" wide, and 1" thick
Packed . . . . single device

Official name . . . . Switch, Demolition; Electric
Circa 1969

THIRTY-DAY CLOCKWORK

DESCRIPTION: The timing and firing mechanism of the Clockwork is enclosed in a machined-metal case. The case has a self-locking metal cap which covers the clock face, dial, and control knobs. A starting and arming knob screw protruding from the side of the case is secured with a cotter safety pin until the clockwork is to be started. The opening in the clockwork base is provided for cocking the mechanism and attaching the military coupling base.

PURPOSE: The Thirty-Day Clockwork is a time-delay mechanism. It is designed to permit the selection of any delayed firing time desired between a MINIMUM of one hour and a MAXIMUM of 720 hours (30 days). The design of the Clockwork enables it to actuate various explosive items; and, when used in conjunction with a special circuit, it can delay the opening or closing of an electric circuit.

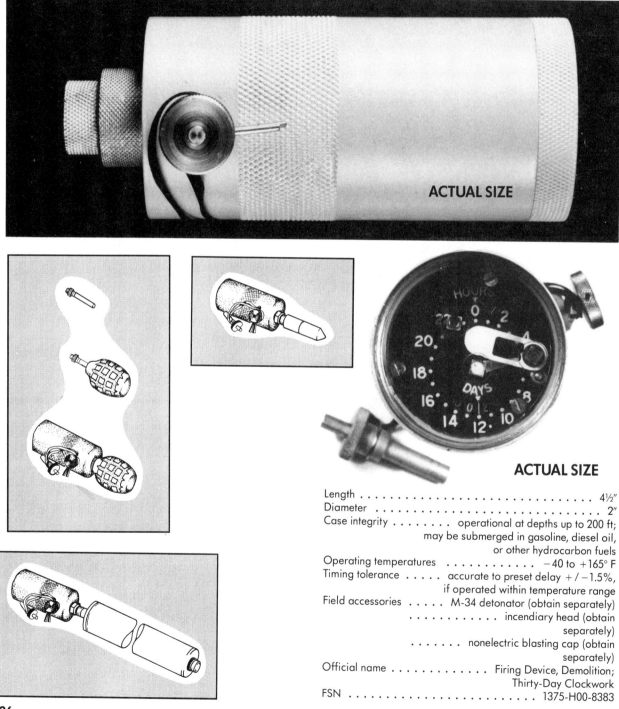

ACTUAL SIZE

ACTUAL SIZE

Length . . . . 4½"
Diameter . . . . 2"
Case integrity . . . . operational at depths up to 200 ft; may be submerged in gasoline, diesel oil, or other hydrocarbon fuels
Operating temperatures . . . . −40 to +165° F
Timing tolerance . . . . . accurate to preset delay +/−1.5%, if operated within temperature range
Field accessories . . . . . M-34 detonator (obtain separately)
. . . . incendiary head (obtain separately)
. . . . nonelectric blasting cap (obtain separately)
Official name . . . . Firing Device, Demolition; Thirty-Day Clockwork
FSN 1375-H00-8383

EXPLOSIVE FLOUR

DESCRIPTION: The Explosive Flour is composition RDX pigmentized (80 percent), wheat flour (20 percent); powder form, five pounds per paper bag.

PURPOSE: This Explosive Flour will pass as ordinary wheat flour except under microscopic examination. It can be used in many different forms as an explosive:

a) in its dry form. The flour is easiest to detonate in its powdered form. One special blasting cap (J1 PETN type) provides sufficient shock to set it off;

b) moistened and used as a plastic explosive. To use as a plastic explosive, mix four parts flour to one part water. It can be moulded around a target in the same manner as Composition C-2, C-3, or C-4. Two special blasting caps (J1 PETN) must be used to ensure positive detonation;

c) it can be mixed with other ingredients to produce ceramic moulding material, or by using a special recipe it can be baked into loaves of bread or biscuits. The product looks, feels, and tastes like bread; however, IT IS HIGHLY TOXIC and SHOULD NOT BE EATEN. Before using the bread form as an explosive, it must be moistened and kneaded into a plastic mass to remove the air spaces. It may then be exploded in the same manner as the plastic form.

Weight . . . . 5 lb and 2 lb bags
Official name . . . . Flour, Explosive; (5 lb or 2 lb bags)
FSN 1475-H00-0005

Explosive Flour can be baked into bread or muffins, or mixed to produce ceramic moulding material.

ANTI-DISTURBANCE MINE

DESCRIPTION: The unit contains a time-delay arming device, sensitive battery-operated firing mechanism, and space for plastic explosive and an electric blasting cap. The plastic explosive and blasting cap are not furnished with the device, but must be obtained and placed in the device by field operators. The unit is prepackaged in a waterproof metal case.

Scale = 1 inch

PURPOSE: The unit is a very sensitive Anti-Disturbance Mine which, when properly loaded and armed, will explode when it is moved or vibrated. Contained within the unit is a time pencil with a minimum delay of ten minutes. After activation of the time pencil the operator has 10–13 minutes before the device is armed.

The mine can be conveniently placed in a wide variety of locations; it has equal sensitivity on all sides. Watertight construction has been used so that the mine can withstand immersion in 20 feet of water for 24 hours. Accessory magnets, not furnished with the mine, may be used to hold the mine in position on metal surfaces. Clamps and screws for use with the accessory magnets are furnished with each mine.

Length . . . . 7"
Width . . . . 4"
Height . . . . 2"
Explosives . . . . 285 grams (13 oz) of plastic explosive; blasting cap (J2 PETN) must be obtained separately
Battery . . . . standard 1.5-V "C" cell (not included)
Official name . . . . Mine, Anti-Disturbance Type
FSN 1345-H00-0010

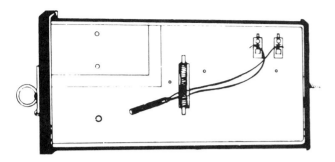

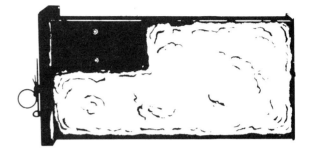

1) Safety test light.

2) Explosive material is moulded to fit inside case.

Caution: The firing mechanism has a tendency to malfunction at subzero temperatures. The mine should not be placed in a structure of such flimsy construction that normal vibration from passing traffic or machinery operating in the area will set it off.

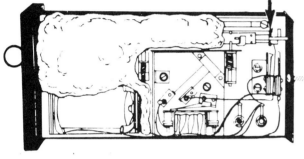

3) Internal detonator.

4) Safety ring.

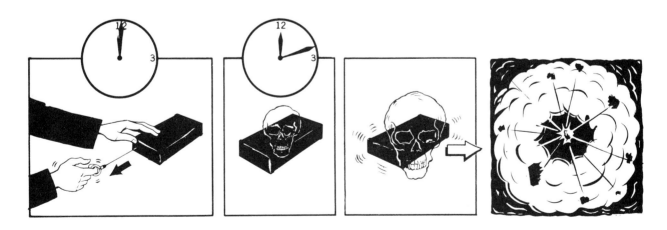

SHAPED DEMOLITION CHARGE

DESCRIPTION: The Shaped Demolition Charge consists of four and one-half ounces of composition RDX in a black moulded plastic case eight inches long and two inches in diameter. The lower five inches of the base is hollow to provide a built-in standoff. One end of a 14-inch length of double-strength Prima cord* is built into the head of the device. Two holes and two studs are provided at the top of the charge to simplify attaching it to the target.

PURPOSE: The Shaped Demolition Charge is capable of punching a hole through seven to ten inches of steel, the hole tapering from one inch at the top to one-quarter inch at the bottom. When used to pierce shafts, bearings, gear boxes, and other crucial parts of machinery, the equipment is put out of operation without destroying the entire machine.

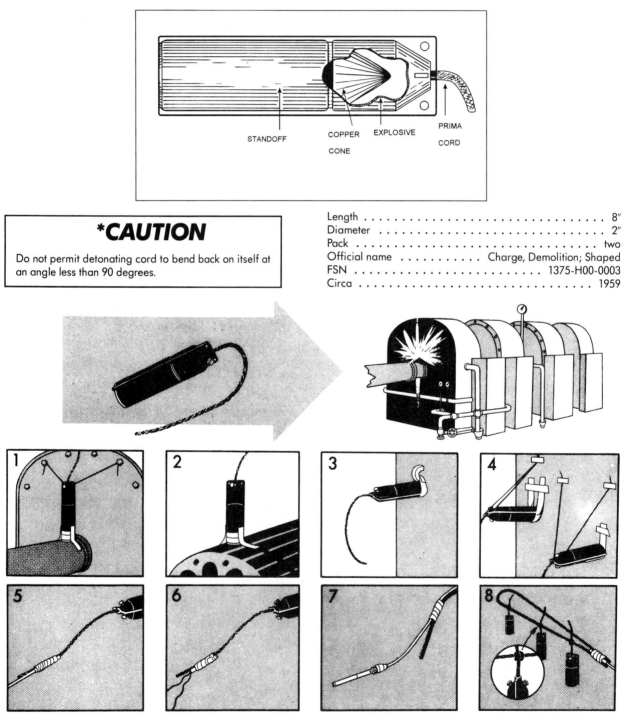

STANDOFF COPPER CONE EXPLOSIVE PRIMA CORD

*CAUTION

Do not permit detonating cord to bend back on itself at an angle less than 90 degrees.

Length . . . . 8″
Diameter . . . . 2″
Pack . . . . two
Official name . . . . Charge, Demolition; Shaped
FSN 1375-H00-0003
Circa 1959

DESCRIPTION: The Gas Tank Charge is in a black plastic case two inches in diameter and one inch thick. Extending from one side is a cylindrical snout into which a blasting cap can be inserted, and on top is a bracket to hold a time pencil or other quick-delay firing device. The charge has a magnet on the bottom permitting quick and secure attachment to a steel fuel tank. The charge is comprised of 28 grams Tetrytol and three and one-half grams incendiary material.

PURPOSE: The Gas Tank Charge is a small explosive—incendiary device which will burst a hole in the fuel tank of a car or truck and ignite the fuel. It also can be used against other fuel containers up to 55-gallon drums. It is not effective against petroleum products less volatile than diesel oil.

Size .... 2" diameter; 1" thick
Packed .... two mines with two detonators; unassembled in metal container
Official name .... Mine, Gas Tank Type
FSN 1345-H00-2631

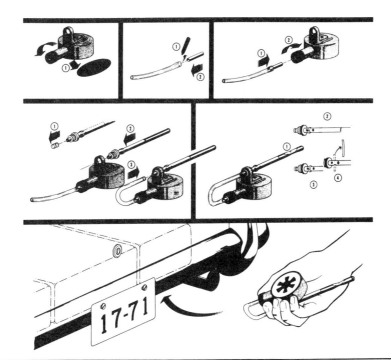

TEMPERATURE CORRECTION TABLE

t °F.	Green OM	Green ST	Yellow OM	Yellow ST	Blue OM	Blue ST	t °C.
−25							−32
0	2.6 day	1.2 day	8.5 day	3.8 day	23 day	10 day	−18
+25	17 hr.	8 hr.	2.0 day	20 hr.	5.0 day	2.2 day	−4
50	6 hr.	2.7 hr.	14 hr.	6.0 hr.	1.3 day	14 hr.	+10
75	2.5 hr.	70 min.	5.5 hr.	2.5 hr.	11.5 hr.	5 hr.	24
100	70 min.	30 min.	2.5 hr.	65 min.	5.2 hr.	2.3 hr.	38
125	35 min.	15 min.	80 min.	36 min.	2.5 hr.	1.1 hr.	52
150	20 min.	9 min.	46 min.	21 min.	80 min.	36 min.	66

OM—When two pencils are used in the same charge, the OM is the most likely timing. When only a single pencil is used, the value should be increased by about 15 percent.

ST—The ST is a reasonably safe time. Timings shorter than the ST should not occur more often than once in a thousand trials.

Red pencils should not be used below 0 degrees F., nor Blue pencils below 25 degrees F.

TEMPERATURE CORRECTION TABLE

t °F.	Black OM	Black ST	Red OM	Red ST	White OM	White ST	t °C.
−25			8.5 hr.	3.3 hr.	3 day	1.3 day	−32
0	8 hr.	2.5 hr.	45 min.	20 min.	17.5 hr.	8 hr.	−18
+25	36 min.	16 min.	25 min.	11 min.	5.5 hr.	2.5 hr.	−4
50	15 min.	7 min.	17 min.	8 min.	2 hr.	55 min.	+10
75	9 min.	4 min.	15 min.	7 min.	1 hr.	27 min.	24
100	5 min.	2.0 min.	8 min.	3.5 min.	32 min.	14 min.	38
125	4 min.	1.5 min.	5 min.	2 min.	20 min.	9 min.	52
150	3 min.	1 min.	4 min.	1.5 min.	15 min.	6 min.	66

OM—When two pencils are used in the same charge, the OM is the most likely timing. When a single pencil is used, the value should be increased by about 15 percent.

ST—The ST is a reasonably safe time. Timings shorter than the ST should not occur more often than once in a thousand trials.

Red pencils should not be used below 0 degrees F., nor Black pencils below 25 degrees F.

GAS TANK PILL

DESCRIPTION: The Gas Tank Pill is contained in a small foil packet. The pill contains compressed fibre strands of various sizes.

PURPOSE: The Gas Tank Pill is designed to disable cars and trucks by disrupting the flow of fuel to the engine. The fibre particles expand when wet and clog the fuel filter and carburetor. The engine will not stop immediately, but will slowly be starved of fuel. The final breakdown will occur miles away from the point of sabotage.

Official name . . . . Sabotage Device, Gas Tank
Circa 1961

BATTERY DESTROYER

DESCRIPTION: The Battery Destroyer kit contains two small plastic bottles of liquid. One bottle is filled with water, and the other with chloroplatinic acid.

PURPOSE: The Battery Destroyer is formulated to discharge wet-storage battery cells. Automobile batteries require an application of ONE drop per cell, while vehicles using larger batteries require TWO drops per cell. Use the water bottle for practice prior to any operational use; THE WATER WILL NOT DAMAGE THE BATTERY. When using the bottle operationally, be certain to replace the caps on each cell after applying the additive. The additive effectively discharges the battery and destroys the cells in four hours or less.

Kit size . . . . 3⅛″ × 3½″ × 1⅛″
Bottle size . . . . 3¼″ × 1½″ × ¾″
Official name . . . . Destructive Device, Battery

Note: **Chloroplatinic acid is caustic, and poisonous. Avoid contact with clothing, skin, eyes, etc.**

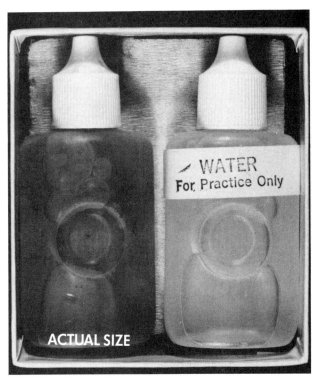

ACTUAL SIZE

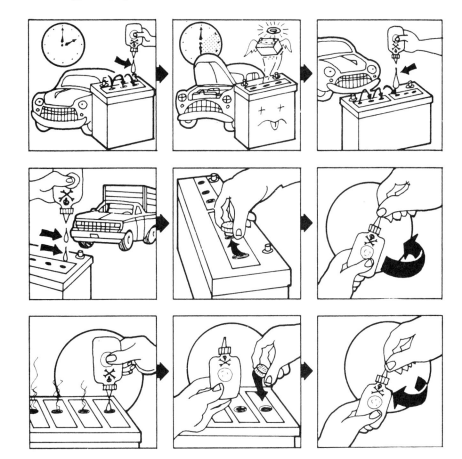

OIL CONTAMINANT

DESCRIPTION: The Oil Contaminant is a one-ounce plastic squeeze bottle attached to a two-foot length of flexible plastic tubing. The bottle contains a powdered abrasive compound that damages and destroys any type of combustion engine.

Official name . . . . Contaminant, Oil
FSN 1365-H06-1051
Circa 1959

PURPOSE: The Oil Contaminant will permanently disable any combustion engine by damaging its pistons, bearings, and cylinder block. The two feet of flexible plastic tubing allow the contents of the bottle to be readily introduced into the engine's oil lubrication system (see diagram). Once the contaminant circulates in the oil supply, it fuses and welds the moving parts of the engine. Total destruction of the engine will occur in approximately one-half hour. The contaminant should be used against all combustion engines, including those found on piston aircraft, tanks, and in factories.

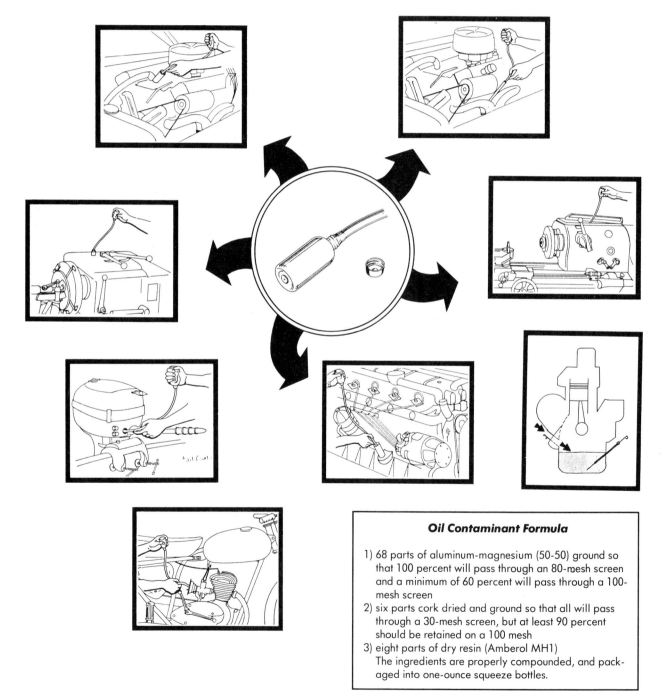

Oil Contaminant Formula

1) 68 parts of aluminum-magnesium (50-50) ground so that 100 percent will pass through an 80-mesh screen and a minimum of 60 percent will pass through a 100-mesh screen
2) six parts cork dried and ground so that all will pass through a 30-mesh screen, but at least 90 percent should be retained on a 100 mesh
3) eight parts of dry resin (Amberol MH1)
The ingredients are properly compounded, and packaged into one-ounce squeeze bottles.

MINIATURE TIRE SPIKE

DESCRIPTION: The Miniature Tire Spike consists of two flat, triangular sections of machined steel slotted to be fitted together. Each tricornered piece has been sharpened, and the area on each side, between the points, has been bevelled into a cutting edge. When assembled, a sharpened point is always upright, and can easily penetrate rubber automotive tires.

PURPOSE: The Miniature Tire Spike is a special version of the standard caltrop designed to be carried in the pocket or purse. The miniature caltrop is used to disable a targeted vehicle by flattening its tire.

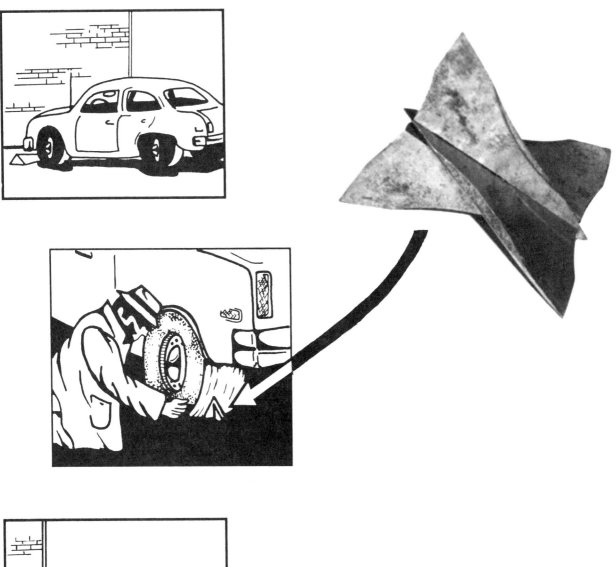

Size . . . . 2″ × 3″
Pack . . . . two pieces
Official name . . . . Destruction Device, Automotive;
                                          Miniature Tire Spike
Circa 1955

TIRE SPIKE

DESCRIPTION: The four-inch-tall Tire Spike is stamped from a single sheet of flat steel and bent into its final shape. Each point is 90 degrees from the horizontal.

PURPOSE: The Tire Spike is designed to puncture rubber tires on both vehicles and airplanes. With their nonreflective finish, the spikes are especially effective when scattered along enemy roads or airfield runways. No matter how the Tire Spike is thrown or dropped, one of its four spikes will land in a vertical, or upright, position.

ACTUAL SIZE

Size . . . . 2" × 3"
Official name . . . Destruction Device, Automotive; Tire Spike
Circa 1965

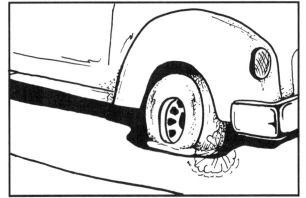

DESCRIPTION: The one and three-quarter-inch-tall Sand Spike consists of a flat, reinforced plastic ring with a sharpened blade extending from each side at a 90-degree angle. Each blade, or spike, is pointed, and sharpened to a razor edge on both sides.

ACTUAL SIZE

Note: The Sand Spike is less effective on conventional hard-surface roads or runways, and should not be used as a substitute for Tire Spikes.

PURPOSE: The conventional Tire Spike is ineffective in sand. The Sand Spike is designed to puncture rubber tires on vehicles operating on sand. The Sand spike works on the same principle as a snowshoe to effectively penetrate rubber tires. The Sand Spike is especially effective when planted so that the circular base is covered with a thin layer of sand, and only the razor-edge blade is exposed. No matter how the Sand Spike is thrown or dropped, one of its two spikes will land in a vertical, or upright, position.

Size . . . . 3¼" diameter; 1¾" high
Official name . . Destruction Device, Automotive; Sand Spike

BLISTER WEAPON

DESCRIPTION: The Blister Weapon consists of a felt-tip applicator and sealed ointment reservoir disguised as a felt-tip marker.

Note: In case of accidental exposure, wash the affected area immediately with an equal mixture of water and Chlorox, Purex, or other five-percent sodium hypochlorite (bleach) solution.

PURPOSE: The Blister Weapon is designed for the surreptitious application of a blister-forming (vesicular) ointment to items that will be handled by a specific individual. Any skin area contacted will be covered in blisters and mordant tissue in 24 hours. Depending on the intensity of exposure, the appearance and intensity of effects may vary. Blistering is nonlethal and will heal within one week.

ACTUAL SIZE

Official name . . . . Vesicular Ointment Applicator; Mark III

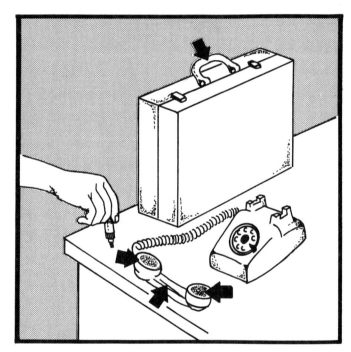

Instructions for Use

1) The applicator will remain inert until activated by pressing the felt tip against a solid surface until the wick breaks through the ointment reservoir seal. The ointment will saturate the applicator in approximately one minute.
2) To apply the blistering agent, the cap is removed and placed on the base of the applicator. The marker wick is then pressed against the surfaces to be contaminated. Only a thin coat is required. There is enough ointment in the applicator to cover 70 square inches.
3) The blistering agent will penetrate most clothing and gloves. Use caution while handling the applicator!

DESCRIPTION: Dust Powder is a small plastic squeeze bottle containing finely powdered tear gas (CS).

PURPOSE: Dust Powder is intended for use as both a harassing agent against crowds and groups of people, as well as a means of personal protection. When Dust Powder comes in contact with the moist tissues of the eyes, nasal passages, or throat, it causes an immediate reaction involving coughing, tears, loss of breath, and nausea. These effects will continue as long as the powder is present. As soon as the person is removed from the contaminated area, the effects disappear in a few minutes.

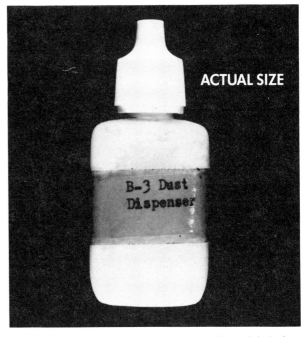

ACTUAL SIZE

B-3 Dust Dispenser

Official name . . . . Harassment Agent; Dust Powder
Circa 1958

Note: Ensure that the cap has been resealed tightly before placing the squeeze bottle back in your pocket or purse.

Using the material against groups involves discharging the contents of the bottle in a factory, office, or outdoor area. To avoid exposure, leave the area as soon as possible. When confronted with an attacker, Dust Powder should be discharged directly into the face.

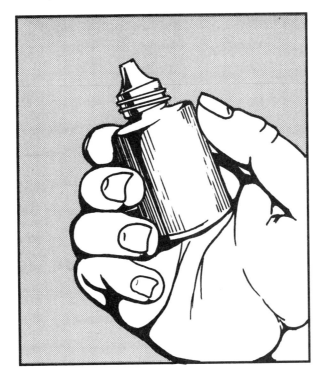

SPD TEAR GAS UNIT

DESCRIPTION: The SPD Tear Gas Unit consists of two basic components: the reusable firing head, and the disposable CS cartridge. The SPD is packaged in a reusable metal container with two (2) inert cartridges, five (5) CS cartridges, and one (1) firing head. The cartridges are individually canned and color coded for ease in identification as follows:

PURPOSE: The small, but powerful SPD Tear Gas Unit is designed to provide operational personnel with the means to disperse small crowds and gatherings, and to force the evacuation of a room or office. The CS gas produced by the cartridge will cause involuntary tearing, coughing, shortness of breath, and nausea.

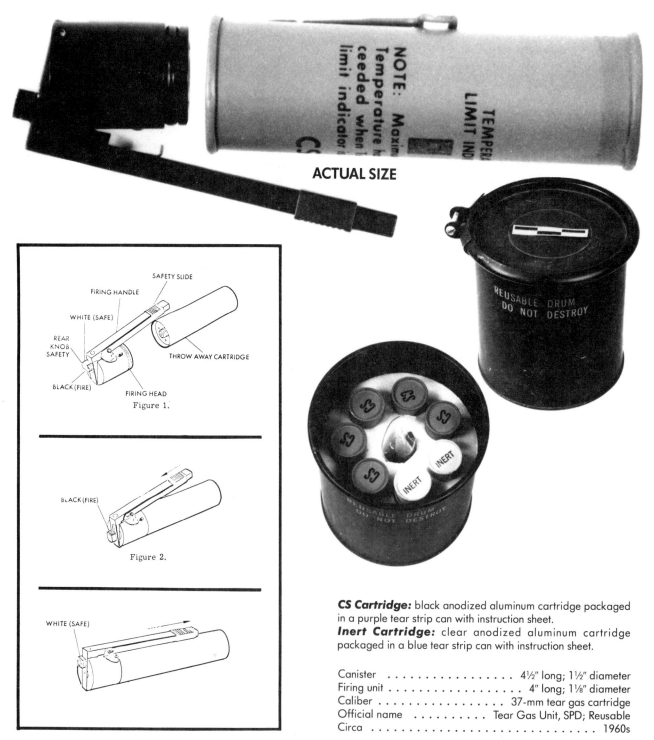

ACTUAL SIZE

Figure 1.

Figure 2.

CS Cartridge: black anodized aluminum cartridge packaged in a purple tear strip can with instruction sheet.
Inert Cartridge: clear anodized aluminum cartridge packaged in a blue tear strip can with instruction sheet.

Canister . . . . 4½" long; 1½" diameter
Firing unit . . . . 4" long; 1⅛" diameter
Caliber . . . . 37-mm tear gas cartridge
Official name . . . . Tear Gas Unit, SPD; Reusable
Circa 1960s

TEAR GAS GUN

DESCRIPTION: The Tear Gas Gun is an aluminum cylinder six and one-half inches long and eleven-sixteenths of an inch in diameter. It contains a quantity of CS gas and a compressed charge. On one end of the device is a plastic tip with a small aperture through which the gas is discharged. The cylinder unscrews in the middle to gain access to the air charge. Both halves of the aluminum cylinder are knurled for ease in handling.

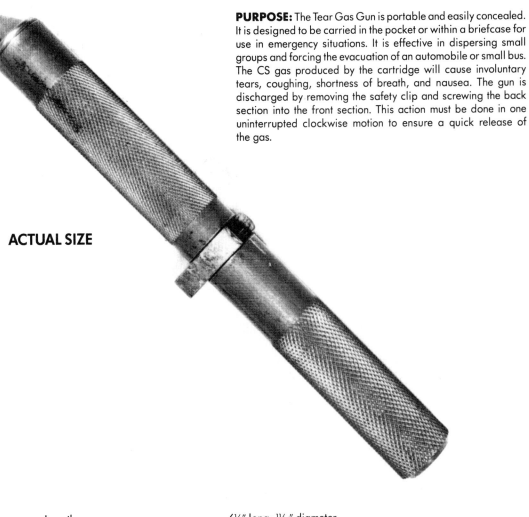

ACTUAL SIZE

PURPOSE: The Tear Gas Gun is portable and easily concealed. It is designed to be carried in the pocket or within a briefcase for use in emergency situations. It is effective in dispersing small groups and forcing the evacuation of an automobile or small bus. The CS gas produced by the cartridge will cause involuntary tears, coughing, shortness of breath, and nausea. The gun is discharged by removing the safety clip and screwing the back section into the front section. This action must be done in one uninterrupted clockwise motion to ensure a quick release of the gas.

Length . . . . 6½" long; ¹¹⁄₁₆" diameter
Discharged by . . . . . . one small, compressed-air cartridge
(Jet Line Gun Co. Inc.)
Official name . . . . Tear Gas Unit, Compressed Air
Circa 1960s

RUBBER AIRPLANE

DESCRIPTION: The Rubber Airplane is a single-place aircraft nearly 20 feet long with a wing span of 28 feet. The craft's one-piece wing, tail assembly, and cockpit are made of two walls of rubberized fabric connected by nylon threads. The plane can operate on land, or on water using a hydroski. Inflation of the aircraft is accomplished by an accompanying pressure bottle.

PURPOSE: The Rubber Airplane allows special personnel to be infiltrated and exfiltrated by air. The pneumatic aircraft may be parachuted into a location and cached until needed. The inflation and assembly operation requires only one man and may be accomplished in less than six minutes. The craft is simple to assemble and easy to fly.

Shown below gaining speed for take-off, hydroski-mounted craft has proved that it can operate on water

Packed with engine, propeller and wheel, the aircraft is inflated by a pressure bottle

Speed .... 70 mph
Range .... 350 miles
Engine .... 40 hp; two-cycle engine
Official name .... Airplane, Pneumatic
Circa 1959

Craft's one-piece wing, tail assembly and cockpit are made of two walls of rubberized fabric connected by nylon threads

POISON NEEDLE

DESCRIPTION: The Poison Needle is a precision, highly machined device 28 centimeters long. It is actually a "needle within a pin." The inner needle is tipped with a lethal poison.

PURPOSE: The curare-tipped Poison Needle is capable of causing death within minutes following introduction of the poison into the bloodstream.

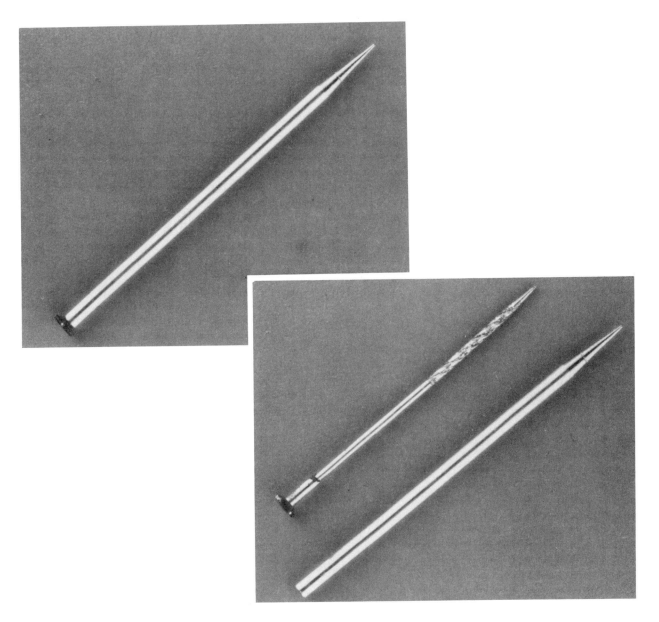

Curare

Curare is extracted from various plants of the *Chondrodendron* family. It has been used by South American Indians for centuries as an arrow poison, because when it enters the bloodstream, it blocks the signals (*acetylcholine*) from nerves to muscles and paralyzes the prey. The muscles involved with respiration are the first to stop working. Death results from asphyxiation.

Needle length . . . . 28 cm
Official name . . . . Needle, Poison
Circa 1960

ONE-MAN SUBMARINE

DESCRIPTION: The One-Man Submarine is an advanced version of the British M.S.C. (Motorized Submersible Canoe) "Sleeping Beauty." The most visible difference is the addition of the two front hydroplanes for greater underwater maneuverability.

The hull can be used as either a surface craft, or submerged to depths in excess of fifty feet. It is thirteen feet long with a twenty-seven-inch beam, and weighs 650 pounds. The craft is equipped with a 24-V 0.4-hp engine powered by four 6-V batteries.

PURPOSE: The One-Man Submarine is used to take operational personnel to a hostile shore from a "mother craft" offshore. The pilot wears a waterproof, cold-resisting, underwater rubber swimsuit, and breathes through a self-contained rebreathing apparatus. The rebreather is preferred over the new self-contained underwater breathing apparatus (SCUBA) gear since the rebreather does not leave a trail of bubbles.

Personnel operating the One-Man Submarines can talk underwater through a special communication system.

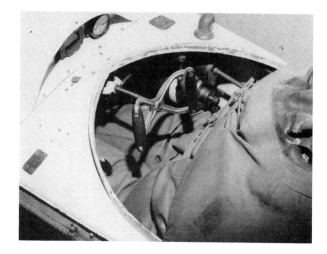

Official name . . . . Submarine, One-Man
Circa 1951
Issued by . . . . US Navy

	Surfaced	Submerged
Cruising speed, knots	3.0	2.0
Full speed, knots	3.5	2.5
Turning radius, yds	35	35
Endurance, cruising, hrs	10	10
Endurance, full speed, hrs	2	2
Range, cruising (miles)	30	25
Range, full speed (miles)	7	5

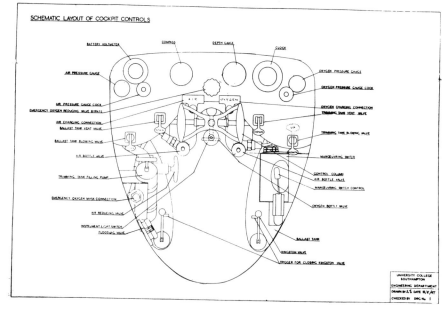

DESCRIPTION: The Disguise Kit is packed within a standard men's toiletry case.

PURPOSE: An effective disguise is one in which your appearance is altered to avoid recognition. Each disguise must fit the situation and be appropriate for the individual involved.

Contained Within Are the Following:

a) shaving or make-up mirror;
b) one tube of facial cream;
c) mustache patterns;
d) preformed mustaches (to be fitted), and small case;
e) spirit gum adhesive;
f) two combs;
g) one small mustache brush;
h) trimming scissors;
i) tweezers;
j) Petri dish, towel, and cotton swabs; and
k) rubber shoe lift for altering wearer's "gait."

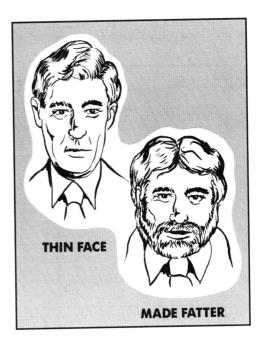

THIN FACE

MADE FATTER

Application of Mustache (MUFF)

1) Clean upper lip with alcohol.
2) Place mustache on upper lip to locate proper position.
3) Apply thin layer of adhesive.
4) Stretch upper lip slightly and gently put muff in place, center first, following line of upper lip. Do not press with fingers, but use teeth of comb. Use water-dampened rag to press upper edges of muff into place.
5) Allow glue to dry for several minutes before moving or stretching lips.
6) Comb and trim muff. Be sure to remove any hair adhering to skin with teeth edge of comb or tweezers.

FAT FACE

MADE THINNER

Case dimensions	11" × 6" × 4"
Weight	16 oz
Official name	Disguise Kit; Facial
Circa	1966

ESCAPE & EVASION SUPPOSITORY

DESCRIPTION: The Escape & Evasion (E&E) Suppository is a portable "tool kit" packed within a waterproof black plastic suppository. Included within the kit are the following:

a) one pair wire cutters, screwdriver, pry bar, and tool handle (in combination);
b) two pointed saw blades;
c) two flat saw blades;
d) one drill;
e) one reamer;
f) one flat file; and
g) one ceramic blade.

PURPOSE: The E&E Suppository packs nine tools in a convenient concealment container. The kit is generally carried in a pocket or briefcase, and should be concealed, rectally, as circumstances require. The tools within the kit are designed to allow a prisoner to free himself from most restraints.

ACTUAL SIZE

ACTUAL SIZE

Length	4"
Width	1" diameter
Official name	Suppository, E & E; Mark I
Circa	1962

FLAPS AND SEALS KIT

DESCRIPTION: The envelope-opening and -resealing kit is in an attaché case, of standard exterior appearance, that has been fitted to contain a surface heater and the necessary adjuncts for its use. The contents are described below:

a) one fitted attaché case with two case keys;
b) one silicon surface heater;
c) two envelopes containing ten blotters;
d) one Teflon sheet, ⅛″ × 8″ × 10″;
e) three plastic (polyethylene) storage bottles;
f) three glass storage bottles;
g) two plastic (polyethylene) pint flasks with one-ounce metal measuring caps;
h) one set of Flaps and Seals (F&S) tools in a cloth roll; and
i) one tube containing ten pressure screws.

PURPOSE: The portable Flaps and Seals Kit, Model 711, is a self-contained unit designed for the manipulation of wax seals, and surreptitious entry into envelopes and other paper conveyances. In the hands of trained personnel it is adequate for entries into highly protected items of mail.

The F&S opening tools are designed for effective openings involving wax seals and envelopes. The silicon heater, or "hamburger grill," is used in conjunction with the blotters (dampened) to provide controlled steam and heat to soften envelope glue. The various plastic containers provide portable supplies of distilled water, glue, and carbon tetrachloride.

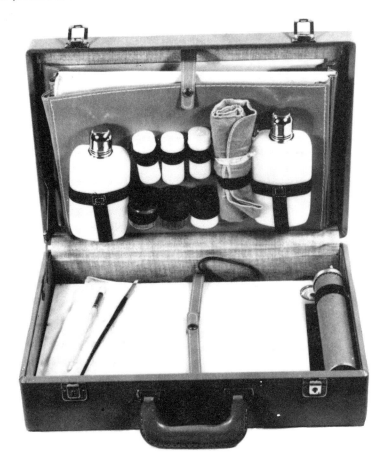

With the tools and equipment provided, the operator is equipped for:

a) dry openings;
b) removal of cellophane tape;
c) wet openings;
d) steam openings;
e) wax seals;
f) repairs (to items damaged during opening);
g) resealing;
h) detection of overt traps; and
i) examination of received mail (for signs of a covert opening).

Height . . . . 5½″
Width . . . . 18″
Depth . . . . 12″
Weight . . . . 12½ lb
Official name . . . . Flaps and Seals Kit; Model 711
Circa 1962

FLAPS AND SEALS TOOL ROLL

DESCRIPTION: The roll contains six specialized tools intended for wet and dry openings of envelopes. The following items are included:

    a) two curved blades (plastic);
    b) two straight blades (plastic);
    c) one straight blade (wood); and
    d) one flat smoothing tool (plastic).

PURPOSE: The majority of all envelope openings can be successfully accomplished through either dry, wet, or steam openings.

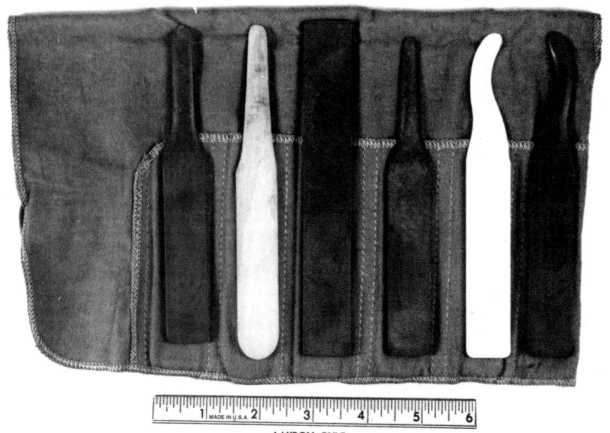

AAKRON RULE

Dry Openings: Wherever possible, the dry method should be used since it is nearly impossible to detect when properly done. A successful dry opening is one where the glue separates into particles or layers, part of which remain on the flap and part on the body of the envelope. If after the initial attempt it is clear that the envelope will not respond, the dry method should be abandoned immediately in favor of the wet or steam opening.

Wet Openings: Many envelopes use water-soluble glue that may be easily softened without damage to the envelope, and opened with the tools provided. Care must be exercised to avoid wetting the ink on the envelope or the letter. Prior to using this method, check for any feathering of ink that may be found along the glue line.

Steam Opening: When no visible evidence exists to indicate that steam or high temperatures will damage the envelope, or the letter, the steam opening is the fastest and most common method of surreptitious openings. Tools are enclosed for steam openings.

Roll length	7" (with flap closed)
Width	1½"
Tool length	6½"
Weight	4 oz
Official name	Tool Roll, Flaps & Seals
Circa	1959

FLAPS AND SEALS HOT PLATE

DESCRIPTION: The Flaps and Seals Hot Plate is a small, all-metal griddle. A variable temperature control dial allows the griddle surface to be set between 100 and 160 degrees F. A POWER light shows when the unit is switched on, and a TEMP light indicates that the griddle surface is at the indicated (as dialed by the user) temperature. The top, front edge of the griddle is a cool, insulated section to allow the user to steady his hands and tools during the opening process. The heating element is protected with a fuse. A spare fuse holder is built into the control panel on the side of the unit.

PURPOSE: The F&S Hot Plate provides a portable heat source for use in the opening of envelopes with steam. It allows the steam to be generated evenly across the entire glued portion of an envelope flap. Relative to the more powerful jet of steam generated by a tea kettle, this evenly distributed steam is potentially less damaging to the fibres of the paper, and may cause less wrinkling of the envelope and letter.

Width . . . . 10"
Height . . . . 5" diameter

Depth . . . . 6"
Power . . . . 300 watts

Instructions for Use

1) Cut a piece of blotting paper to the size of the top of the "grill" being used, and wet it by flowing water across its surface. (Do not soak the blotter!)
2) Lay the blotter on the "grill" and increase the temperature until steam can barely be seen rising from the surface of the blotter. This temperature varies with altitude, and should be set through trial-and-error on nonoperational material.
3) The envelope is placed flap down on the blotter. If the envelope corners begin to curl, they should be lightly held down with wooden depressors.
4) After 15–30 seconds, lift the bottom of the envelope and see if the point of the flap is loose by pulling it down with gentle pressure from an opening tool.
5) If it is loose, hold the tip gently against the blotter with the opening tool and lift the envelope up. It should open easily. If it does not, leave it for a few more seconds and try again.

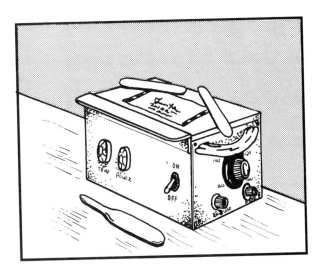

Official name . . . . Flaps and Seals Hot Plate; Model-1
Circa 1949

DEAD DROP DEVICE

DESCRIPTION: This Dead Drop Device is an aluminum cylinder with one pointed end. The reverse end may be opened by unscrewing the knurled cap. The cavity within the tube is protected from moisture and water by a rubber gasket.

PURPOSE: A Dead Drop is a device in which personnel may communicate by leaving and picking up material, thereby eliminating the need for direct contact. Typically, Dead Drops are used for the transfer of signal plans, ciphered messages, film cassettes, etc.

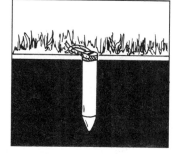

Dead Drop devices can be improvised (such as using an empty soda can) or specially constructed for hiding in certain types of locations. This cylindrical Dead Drop is designed for use in grassy areas such as public parks or wooded areas. Once "planted," it is effectively hidden unless you know exactly where to look. Due to its watertight seal, it may be utilized in unconventional locations such as a shallow stream bed or coastal area.

The cylindrical Dead Drop is available in different sizes to accommodate various types of material and comes in various colors for camouflage.

ACTUAL SIZE

Dimensions . . . . larger, 6¼" × ⅞"
. . . . smaller, 5¼" × ½"
Colors . . . . available in black and olive drab
Official name . . . . Concealment Chamber, Cylindrical
Circa 1969

DESCRIPTION: The device is a standard-appearing coin of the type to be found in circulation within the country selected. Other than a slight variation in weight (lower), there are no external signs that the coin has been modified. The coin has been machined from two authentic coins and may be opened only by applying pressure at a specified point on one side of the coin. Once opened, the two halves separate and reveal a small concealment cavity.

ACTUAL SIZE

PURPOSE: The hollow coin allows the bearer to utilize a small concealment cavity that will safely withstand a cursory physical examination. When carried with other similar, but unmodified, coins, the hollow coin is effectively camouflaged. Depending on the coin selected, the chamber is of sufficient size to hold individual frames of 35-mm film, microdots, signal plans, Skeds, etc.

Dimensions . . . . vary with denomination and country of coin selected

Official name . . . . . Coin, Hollow; (coin requested must be specified)

HOLLOW SHAVING CAN

DESCRIPTION: The Hollow Shaving Can has been modified from an ordinary can of aerosol shaving cream. It is identical in appearance and "feel" to the standard, commercially available product. Access to the concealment cavity is achieved by rotating the base of the unit. The threads on the can have been reversed so that the normal (clockwise) rotation of the base for opening will make the concealment more secure. The aerosol can is functional.

PURPOSE: The Hollow Shaving Can is a small, portable, concealment cavity. When camouflaged with the toiletry items normally found in a man's shaving kit, it will pass most luggage examinations unnoticed. The cavity is intended for the concealment and transport of:

a) film (exposed or unexposed);
b) radio communications schedules (Skeds);
c) cipher material;
d) secret writing chemicals;
e) currency; and
f) notes and documents.

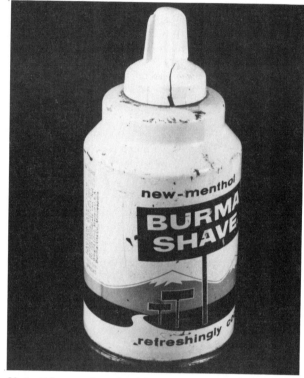

Length	6"
Width	3" diameter
Cavity	1½" deep; 3" diameter
Threads	reverse (clockwise to open)
Official name	Concealment Chamber, Aerosol Spray; brand and country of origin must be specified individually.
Circa	1965

Note: This aerosol can should be the only shaving cream carried in the luggage. For maximum effectiveness, the can should show signs of prior use, and be packed with a razor (nonelectric).

DESCRIPTION: The desk is constructed in a style and manner to blend with other furniture within the area in which it will be utilized. Hidden within the desk is a concealment chamber (cavity) that can only be opened by sliding a piece of moulding to release a concealed latch.

PURPOSE: The special desk provides a concealment chamber for the secret storage of weapons, manuals, cameras, explosives, etc. The desk has been selected and modified in such a manner that the concealment chamber will pass unnoticed unless it is subjected to a close examination. The release latch is located in a position that requires special effort to reach and activate.

Similar concealments may be constructed in end tables, chests of drawers, file cabinets, etc. The space required and the style of furniture to be used will determine the final configuration of the concealment. Each piece of furniture is individually crafted or modified for the application specified at time of order.

Desk length	47"
Desk height	32"
Desk width	28"
Cavity width	4½"
Cavity height	25¼"
Cavity depth	18"
Wood	as required
Circa	1968
Official name	(special order only)

Desk with concealment chamber opened.

DOG REPELLENT

DESCRIPTION: The hermetically sealed outer can holds a smaller aerosol cylinder containing a special gas that causes instant, but temporary, irritation and stinging to a dog's eyes. A standard household style "twist opener" is provided.

PURPOSE: The special dog repellent gas has a maximum effective range of six feet. Wherever possible, it is recommended that the dog be sprayed while the user is protected behind a fence or gate. The spray has an instant reaction as soon as it reaches the dog's eyes. Though the reaction is temporary, one application will usually be sufficient to discourage the animal's interest in your activities.

Note: Do not attempt to ward off guard or sentry dogs with standard-issue "tear gas," or CS. Tests have shown these gases to be ineffective against dogs.

Official name . . . . Dog Repellent; Spray
Circa 1970

DESCRIPTION: Puppy Chow consists of:

a) one plastic case containing 20 tranquilizer capsules; and
b) two syrettes containing antidote.

PURPOSE: Puppy Chow is used to silence guard dogs by feeding them the tranquilizer capsules mixed with ground beef. Though the correct portion for the average guard dog is four capsules, it may be increased if the animal's ferocity warrants.

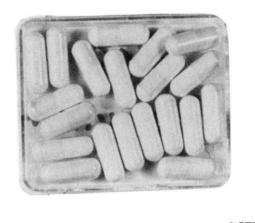

ACTUAL SIZE

The animal will be rendered unconscious for up to four hours. The effects of the tranquilizer are only temporary; the dog will suffer no aftereffects other than loss of balance and lethargy during the recovery period. Should it be needed, a syrette filled with antidote may be injected to speed up the animal's recovery.

Tranquilizer . . . . 20 capsules
Antidote . . . . two syrettes
Official name . . . . Tranquilizer, Capsule; Dog
Circa 1963

BLACK BOOK

DESCRIPTION: The Black Book is a small and easily concealed, six-ring, loose-leaf notebook.

Width closed . . . . 5¼"
Height . . . . 7¼"
Language . . . . English only
Official name . . Instructional Manual, Improvised Explosives
Circa 1962

PURPOSE: The Black Book is intended to provide operational personnel with the technical information necessary to improvise munitions and other expedient devices in the field. This information may be useful in the absence of conventional supplies, or for instructing indigenous personnel. The techniques shown are easily learned (or taught), and require only commonly available ingredients.

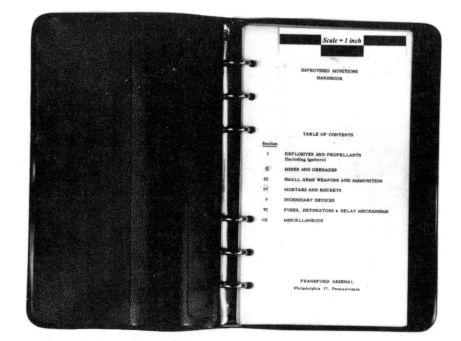

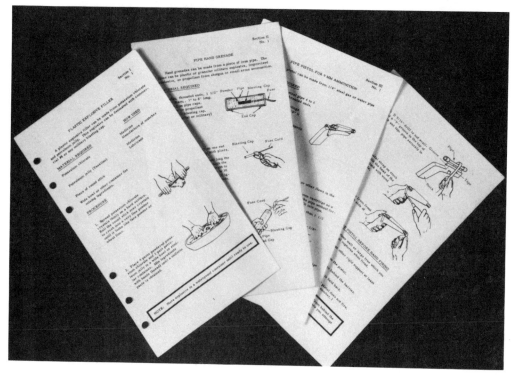

DESCRIPTION: This small, low-cost manual contains information on simple, but effective, techniques for waging psychological and guerrilla warfare.

PURPOSE: The important psychological and guerrilla warfare techniques presented are intended for use in destroying the economic infrastructure that any government needs in order to function. With only an investment of resources and time this necessary infrastructure may be disabled and effectively paralyzed. Manuals should be distributed in large numbers to encourage the widespread utilization of the information and techniques presented.

Size . . . . 5″ × 6⅝″
Language . . . . Spanish
Circa 1983

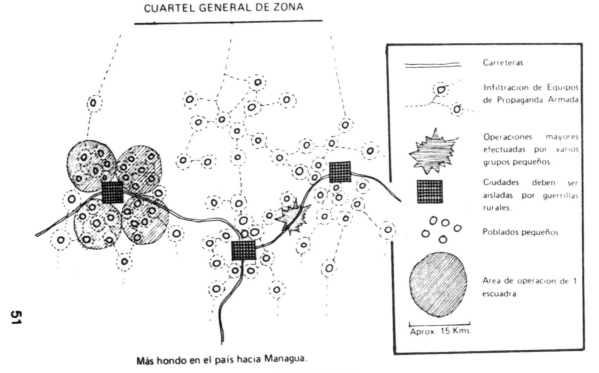

CUARTEL GENERAL DE ZONA

Carreteras

Infiltracion de Equipos de Propaganda Armada

Operaciones mayores efectuadas por varios grupos pequeños.

Ciudades deben ser aisladas por guerrillas rurales.

Poblados pequeños

Area de operacion de 1 escuadra

Aprox. 15 Kms.

Más hondo en el país hacia Managua.

ACTUAL SIZE

IDENTI-KIT

DESCRIPTION: The Identi-Kit consists of a clear-plastic container, transparent pictorial slides, and a handbook. The 2¼" × 3½" slides contain variations of the following characteristics:

a) age lines;
b) beards and mustaches;
c) chin lines;
d) eyes;
e) eyebrows;
f) face colors;
g) glasses;
h) hair;
i) headgear;
j) lips;
k) noses; and
l) scar grid

PURPOSE: Surveillance photographs are sometimes unavailable for subjects of possible operational interest. The Identi-Kit system allows such individuals to be identified based solely on recognizable facial characteristics. These facial characteristics may be selected from the slide categories enclosed for any face. When properly assembled, according to the handbook provided, they will form a line drawing representative of a full face view of the subject. This drawing may, of necessity, be constructed following only a single observation.

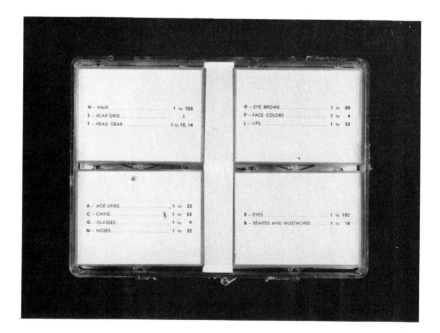

H — HAIR	1 to 102	
S — SCAR GRID	1	
T — HEAD GEAR	1 to 12, 14	
D — EYE BROWS	1 to 80	
F — FACE COLORS	1 to 4	
L — LIPS	1 to 33	
A — AGE LINES	1 to 23	
C — CHINS	1 to 52	
G — GLASSES	1 to 9	
N — NOSES	1 to 32	
E — EYES	1 to 102	
B — BEARDS AND MUSTACHES	1 to 18	

Case dimensions . . . . 7½" × 5½" × 2"
Slide size . . . . 2¼" × 3½"
Official name . . . . Identi-Kit
Circa 1960

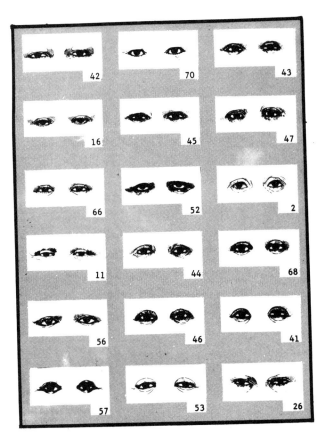

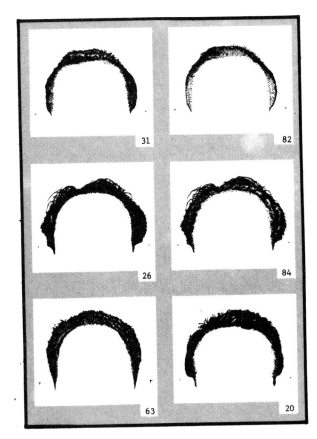

Persons involved in surveillance operation should learn special observation habits. Faces should be viewed as components, and not as indistinct characteristics that form the face as a whole. The following sequence should be adopted in establishing proper patterns of observation:

1) Establish presence, or absence, of age lines, wrinkles and scars, or marks.
2) Memorize the hairline.
3) Observe the eyes and eyebrows.
4) Notice the size, shape, and length of the nose.
5) View the size, shape, and "mouth line" of the mouth.
6) Memorize the chin as to size, shape, and contour.

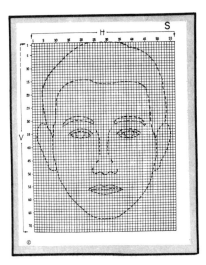

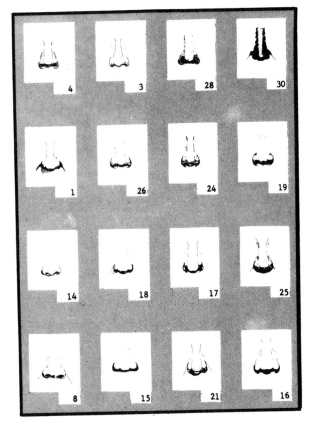

Overseas Careers

Knowledge is the core of our nation's security

Prudent foreign policy decisions depend on solid knowledge. The most important decisions depend on information our adversaries seek to conceal. A truly extraordinary group of men and women serve abroad as the key players in our national effort to fill these critical information gaps. If you measure up, you may join this group and enjoy an exceptional career.

The Standard: Total professionalism. An Agency career is a vocation, a way of life, not a conventional routine.

The Task: Serve throughout the world, working with foreign nationals at all levels. Develop the skills and professional discipline to produce results in conditions of stress and, on occasion, personal risk.

The Reward: The satisfaction of meeting and mastering exceptional challenge. Having an answer to the question: How can I help serve my country's future? The prospect of adventure while doing a job that calls on the deepest resources of intelligence, professional skills, and personal commitment.

The Qualifications: Above everything else, the drive to achieve. Force of personality and a gift for dealing with people combine with intercultural sophistication to assure effectiveness anywhere in the world. A high level of academic performance and first-rate communication skills facilitate a command of complicated matters of intelligence substance. These skills are also essential to the preparation of lucid, accurate reporting. A good aptitude for foreign languages ensures rapid progress toward fluency in Agency language training. Solid ethical standards guarantee the integrity of performance in activities as sensitive as they are important.

Do you measure up? If you have the skills, desire, and discipline, you may qualify for selection into our intensive entry-level training program. Send a resume and a letter describing the qualities which equip you to meet the challenge we offer. Include day and evening phone numbers, please. We will respond to WRITTEN inquiries only. Entrance salaries range from $22,000 to $34,000 depending on credentials. Substantial premium for service abroad. College graduates with a minimum of a Bachelor's degree and U.S. citizens only. Maximum age 35.

Jay A. Collingswood
Dept. S, Rm. 4N20 (H30)
P.O. Box 1925
Washington, D.C. 20013

Central Intelligence Agency

The CIA is an Equal Opportunity Employer

Post-Cold War recruiting ad placed by the CIA.

CIA Medals, Identification
Cards, Credentials, and Badge

DISTINGUISHED INTELLIGENCE CROSS
For Extraordinary Heroism

DISTINGUISHED INTELLIGENCE MEDAL
For Outstanding Service

INTELLIGENCE STAR
For Courageous Action

INTELLIGENCE MEDAL OF MERIT
For Meritorius Service

CAREER INTELLIGENCE MEDAL
For Exceptional Achievement

INTELLIGENCE COMMENDATION MEDAL
For Especially Commendable Services

EXCEPTIONAL SERVICE MEDALLION
For Injury or Death in the
Performance of Hazardous Duties

GOLD RETIREMENT MEDALLION
35 Years of Agency Service

SILVER RETIREMENT MEDALLION
25 Years of Agency Service

BRONZE RETIREMENT MEDALLION
15 Years of Agency Service

Identification credentials of Allen W. Dulles—Director of Central Intelligence, 1953–1961.

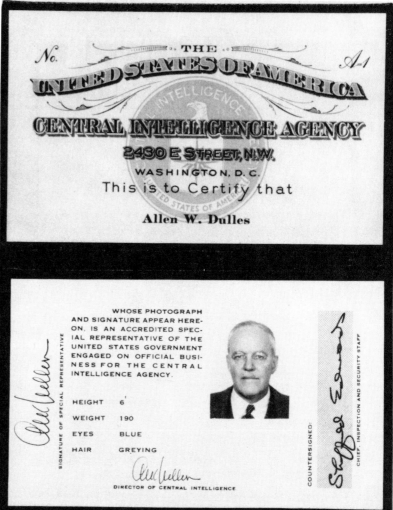

Early badge worn by uniformed personnel patrolling the grounds around CIA facilities.

Identification card of CIA officer James Angleton.

Clandestine Audio Operations

Clandestine audio operations circa 1960 involved the skills of telephone tapping and techniques of electronic surveillance, or "bugging."

The easiest and most reliable method of telephone tapping was a formal request of the local telephone company, made through the intelligence service liaison of the friendly "host" country. If this was not possible, techniques were taught that allowed the target's telephone to be tapped along the line between his phone and the exchange. This tap might be either a direct-wire connection to the line, or an inductive coupling that required no connection. The CIA Technical Services Division (TSD) also built small radio frequency transmitters that could be attached at any point to the telephone wires, and transmitted to a listening post (LP) nearby.

Telephones and telephone lines were used for the audio penetration of rooms in which they were located. So-called "hot mikes" allowed the telephone to remain on the receiver, but permitted normal conversation in the room to be transmitted along the line to an LP.

The basic form of "bugging" is the simple "mike-and-wire" installation. A microphone is concealed within the target room, and two wires are run to the LP, where an amplifier and tape recorder are located. While this type of equipment requires more extensive access to the site for installation, it is secure from counterintelligence "audio-sweeps" since it transmits along the wires and not on a radio frequency. The weakness is in the difficulty of hiding the wires as they run to the LP. "Mike-and-wire" operations were favored in locations in which permanent audio operations were required, and which allowed frequent access for installation, such as "safe houses" or rooms in "friendly" hotels used regularly by foreign visitors.

To avoid the problems with running wires to the LP, it was possible to connect the "mike-and-wire" to a low-powered radio transmitter for reception at the LP. The transmitters could be powered by regular house current, or batteries. Remotely controlled on/off switches for the transmitters were necessary to avoid detection

by audio-sweep teams using wideband receivers to search for illicit transmissions. The Soviets, and their satellite countries, frequently rotated counterintelligence technical teams through their embassies and consulates around the world in an effort to ferret out "bugs."

Battery power for transmitters located within a hostile target was a continuing problem. Newly developed (in 1960) transistorized components required less power than earlier vacuum tubes, but the life expectancy of an audio installation was limited unless batteries could be replaced. Replacement usually entailed either a dangerous reentry into the target area, or the cooperation of a person (such as a friendly foreign national who had been co-opted into service) with access to the area.

Many of the drawbacks of both systems were solved by using a technique called carrier-current transmitters. These installations were similar to regular transmitters, except that the power was drawn from household current and the audio signal was transmitted along the line and not into the air. This allowed for on/off switching, unlimited power supply, and safety from audio-sweep teams. The major drawback was that the signal transmitted along the line would not pass through a power transformer. As

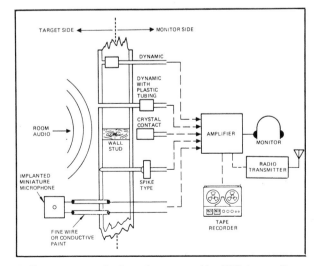

Different types of microphones used by TSD to monitor conversations through a wall.

a result, installations were limited to those areas in which an LP could be situated between the installation and the first power transformer.

The installation of microphones in a target room was an area of specialty for TSD. An impressive array of drills and accessories were developed to aid in the installation of unseen microphones. A hole was drilled into the floor, wall, or ceiling of sufficient size to hold the microphone, but not going all the way through. A successful installation required only a final opening of pinhole size in the target room through which sound could travel. A variety of microphones of different types and design allowed the installer to select the optimum equipment for each installation. After the microphone was in place, a special camouflage kit was provided that aided in patching and painting the wall to hide any visible signs of the installation. Similar techniques were used to hide the presence of the wires as they were run from the microphone to the transmitter, or directly to the LP.

Within the LP were usually a reel-to-reel tape recorder (Revere was popular in the early 1960s, and later replaced by Ampex) and an actuator that turned on the recorder when the telephone set was in use or when there were voices near an active transmitter. The signal reached the LP either by wires, or if transmitted, via a multipurpose radio receiver, such as the SRR-4.

The research and development program of the TSD Audio Branch worked continuously for:

1) development of smaller and more sensitive microphones;
2) more effective ways to turn remote switch transmitters on and off;
3) flat long-life batteries (called "poker chips");
4) innovative ways to conceal microphones and transmitters in everyday-appearing items such as electrical plugs, wall outlets, and pieces of furniture, etc.;
5) advanced concepts (for 1960) that bounced infrared beams off target windows and modulated the reflection from the window pane as it vibrated from voices within the room; and
6) new techniques in passive cavity transmitters that were based on the design of the Soviet microphone found hidden in the Great Seal of the United States hanging above the Ambassador's desk in Moscow. This design required no internal power, and was activated by a radio signal.

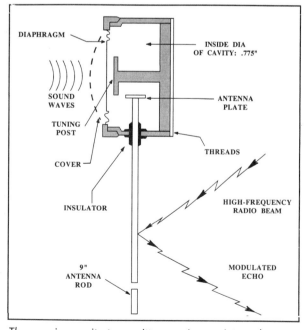

The passive cavity transmitter requires no internal power. It is energized by a high-frequency radio beam aimed at the device.

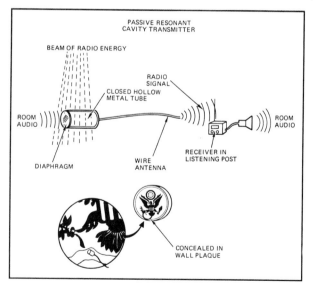

Passive cavity transmitter found in the American Embassy, Moscow, was a "gift" from the Soviets. The CIA was startled to discover the advanced technology being used by the Soviets for eavesdropping in this 1952 discovery. The device transmitted on a frequency of 330 MHz.

Glossary

Agency, the A name for the CIA used, casually, by employees and other members of the intelligence community

Agent Usually used to refer to a foreign national in the employ of the intelligence agency. CIA employees are not "agents," but rather officers

Agent Transmitter Small radio transmitter concealed on a person's body used for protection or consensual monitoring

Antibug Radio noise generator designed to interfere with "bugs"

Audio Monitoring Electronic device or devices designed and used to listen to conversations, sometimes from a remote point

Back Channels Separate communication channel(s) used by CIA for clandestine messages that bypass conventional embassy, or other "official," procedures and frequencies

Blackbox Any type of technical spying device or equipment

Black Ops Any type of activities or operations that are, by intention, not traceable back to the agency

Bubble, the An acoustically insulated space in which secrets can be discussed safely. The "bubble" is constructed in such a way that it prevents the use of enemy audio listening devices

Bug Clandestine listening device; usually a small radio transmitter connected to a miniature microphone

Bug Detector Electronic audio countermeasures device used to locate "bugs"

Bugging Process of monitoring conversations by electronic means

Bumper Beeper Radio beacon transmitter hidden in or on a vehicle for use with radio-locating equipment

Burst A technique in which a coded message is compressed, and then broadcast at high speed. A base station can record the burst signal and play it back at a reduced speed to recover the original message. Used to avoid enemy direction-finding techniques

Bury To hide a message within another communication; or to conceal, as in "burying" a microdot

Carbon Microphone A telephone transmitter that depends on the variation of carbon granules for its operation

Case Officer An officer of an intelligence agency involved in the collection of intelligence

Cavity Resonator Type of microwave transducer or reflector that modulates a received microwave beam in the presence of audio frequencies

Charge, Shaped A mass of high-explosive having a shaped metallic recess that causes it to have a one-way penetrating action known as "Munroe" effect. Used to blast holes in steel, concrete, or similar materials

Cheese Box An electronic device connected between two telephone lines to prevent calls from being traced

CIA Central Intelligence Agency

Clandestine Services Referring to intelligence organizations involved in secret intelligence gathering. This would include, but not be limited to, CIA, NSA, DIA, etc.

Company, the A casually used name for the CIA

Consensual Monitoring Description of legal situation wherein conversations between two individuals are monitored with the knowledge of one of the participants

Contact Microphone A specially constructed microphone designed to be attached directly to the surface to be monitored. This type of microphone generally responds only when the object or surface is vibrated

Countermeasures Defensive techniques designed to detect, prevent, or expose the use of electronic, audio, or visual surveillance devices; Sweeping

Crystal Microphone A microphone that depends for its operation on the generation of an electric charge by the deformation of a crystal

CS Tear gas agent

DCI Director of Central Intelligence

Dead Babies False identification documents used to support a "cover"

Dead Drop A place or device in which messages (or other material) can be left. Using a "Dead Drop" removes the need for direct contact between personnel

D/Fing Direction finding (see Triangulation)

DIA Defense Intelligence Agency

Direct Current (DC) Current provided by batteries

Directional Microphone A microphone that is extremely sensitive to audio frequencies arriving from one direction, while rejecting those from other directions

Drop-in Mouthpiece A telephone radio tap transmitter concealed in a case that has the appearance of a carbon telephone mouthpiece

Eavesdropping Secretly listening to or recording conversations; includes both bugging and wiretapping

Electronic Stethoscope Contact microphone or physician's stethoscope equipped with an electronic amplifier

Executive Action A euphemism for assassination

ELINT Electronic Intelligence

Farm, the Main CIA training facility outside of Williamsburg, Virginia

Field Strength Meter An electronic radio field strength detection device that detects the presence of R-F energy

Firestarter An item containing flammable material, designed to start fires under adverse weather conditions where other methods would fail

Firing Device A mechanism designed to detonate the main charge of explosives contained in booby traps, antipersonnel mines, antitank mines, and demolition charges. There are several types: pressure, pull, release, or combination thereof

Flaps & Seals (F&S) Tradecraft terminology for the opening (and later closing) of sealed documents and letters

Gammas Another name for One-Time Pads

Hardwire Use of wire pair rather than radio transmitter to communicate information between two points

Hood Switch Switch-in telephone instrument actuated by the plunger or bracket on which the handset rests when not in use

Honey Trap An operation intended to sexually compromise an opponent

Hot Mike Activation of the microphone of a telephone in the "hung up" position through use of a third wire, silicon rectifier, or other electronic components

HUMINT Human Intelligence

Infinity Bug An audio amplifier and microphone connected to a telephone line through an audio-tone sensitive relay which is activated by telephoning the bugged premises and sounding the coded tone

Infrared (IR) Light waves too low in frequency to be seen by the human eye; produced by thermal radiation

Invisible Ink One of the ways in which Secret Writing (SW)

messages may be sent. The ink is visible when written, but dries to leave no trace. The message becomes visible again only when treated with a special developer

"L" Pill   Lethal pill

Listening Post   Location where technicians monitor receiving equipment during bugging operations

Microdot   Produced through a photographic process which reduces a page of type to an image the size of the period following this sentence. The image is invisible to the unaided human eye. Technically, a microdot refers to a reduction of greater than 1:200

Mikrat   A reduction of a page of type to a tiny rectangle of film smaller than microfilm, but not as small as a microdot

Monitor   Radio receiver used to monitor clandestine transmissions

One-Time Pad   A pad with a series of random numbers printed on each page. These numbers are used only once to encipher a message that is unbreakable

Optical Fibres   Special glass fibres used to carry light

OSS   Office of Strategic Services

OTS   Office of Technical Services; successor to TSD as the creator of tradecraft equipment for the CIA

Parabolic Microphone   Microphone with large disk-like attachment used for listening to audio from great distances

PHOTINT   Photographic Intelligence

Q Devices   A camouflaged tradecraft device. The name originated with the "Q" ships of World War I

Quick Plant   Audio bugging transmitter easily installed or dropped in target area

RDX   Cyclonite (explosive)

Ricin   A highly lethal poison derived from the castor bean

Sabotage   An intentional act of destruction. May be aimed at the economy of a nation, or against a factory or individual piece of equipment

Secret Writing (SW)   Making messages disappear so they may be transmitted as part of a letter of standard appearance

Silent Rooms   Areas shielded acoustically against eavesdropping

Skeds   Radio communications schedules

Snuggling   A technique used in which the frequency of a clandestine, low-power audio transmitter is "snuggled" adjacent to a more powerful local radio station frequency. If the room is "swept" for bugs, the detection equipment will usually pick up the powerful local station and miss the low-power transmitter

Soft Film   A technique through which the emulsion of the film is separated from the much thicker backing. The emulsion can then be rolled or compressed and hidden

Spike Mike   Contact microphone with a long needle-like extension used for listening through walls

Spy Dust   Special chemical placed on the shoes or clothing of an individual and used to trace movements

Suppresser   A device that attaches to, or is built into, a pistol or rifle for the purpose of reducing its sound signature upon firing. Sometimes referred to as a "silencer"

Surveillance   Secretly observing the behavior of another; includes both audio eavesdropping and visual monitoring

Surveillance Receiver   Radio receiver used to monitor radio transmitter bugs or beacons

Target   An individual under surveillance; can also be a factory, company, country, or any object of an intelligence operation

Tea & Biscuit Co.   Slang expression used when referring to the CIA

Tear Gas   A substance, usually liquid, which, when atomized and of a certain concentration, causes temporary but intense eye irritation and a blinding flow of tears in anyone exposed to it. Also called a "lacrimator"

Technical Surveillance   Bugging, wiretapping, televising, or radio tracking techniques

TOPS   Technical Operating Specialist (CIA)

Toys   Casual expression referring to tradecraft devices and equipment

Tradecraft   Organized and systematized techniques and practices of clandestine behavior. Includes both the specialized "tools" of espionage, as well as the skills necessary to use them

Triangulation   Process used to locate a beacon by use of multiple direction-finding receivers

Trigram   Method of designating CIA equipment using a three-letter code (such as "SRR")

TSD   Technical Services Division (CIA); this division produced the specialized pieces of tradecraft equipment used in clandestine operations. TSD was later changed to OTS (Office of Technical Services)

TSS   Technical Services Staff (CIA)

Watchers, the   British term for persons who are trained for, and regularly conduct, physical surveillance

Wiretap   Clandestine interception of a telephone conversation away from the target premises

Bibliography

Agee, Philip. *Inside the Company: CIA Diary.* New York: Stonehill, 1975.

Emanuel, W.D. *Minox Guide: How to Get the Best Out of the Minox A, B, C and BL.* New York: Focal Press, 1974.

Kahn, David. *The Codebreakers: The Story of Secret Writing.* New York: The Macmillan Company, 1967.

Kennedy, Col. William V. *Intelligence Warfare: Penetrating the Secret World of Today's Advanced Technology Conflict.* New York: Crescent, 1983.

Ladd, James, and H. Keith Melton. *Clandestine Warfare: Weapons and Equipment of the SOE and OSS.* London: Blandford Press, 1988.

Lapin, Lee. *How to Get Anything On Anybody, Book II: The Encyclopedia of Personal Surveillance.* San Mateo, CA: ISECO, Inc., 1992.

MacInaugh, Edward A. *Disguise Techniques.* Secaucus, NJ: Citadel Press, 1988.

McLean, Donald B. *The Plumber's Kitchen: The Secret Story of American Spy Weapons.* Wickenberg, AZ: Normount Technical Publications, 1975.

Melton, H. Keith. *OSS Special Weapons and Equipment: Spy Devices of WWII.* New York: Sterling Publishing Co., 1991.

Minnery, John. *CIA Catalog of Clandestine Weapons, Tools, and Gadgets.* Boulder, CO: Paladin Press, 1990.

———— *Fingertip Firepower: Pen Guns, Knives, and Bombs.* Boulder, CO: Paladin Press, 1990.

Paladin Press. *CIA Explosives Supply Catalog.* Paladin Press (no date).

———— *CIA Special Weapons Supply Catalog.* Paladin Press (no date).

———— *Sabotage and Demolition Manual.* Paladin Press (no date).

Peake, Hayden. *The Reader's Guide to Intelligence Periodicals.* Washington, DC: NIBC Press, 1992.

Pollock, David A. *Methods of Electronic Audio Surveillance.* Springfield, IL: Thomas, 1973.

Ranelagh, John. *The Agency: The Rise and Decline of the CIA.* Great Britain: Hodder and Stoughton, Ltd., 1988.

Telecommunication Publishing Inc. *Protecting Your Privacy.* Telecommunication Publishing Inc. (no date).

Tobias, Marc Weber. *Locks, Safes, and Security: A Handbook for Law Enforcement Personnel.* Springfield, IL: Thomas, 1971.

US Government. *CIA Fact Book on Intelligence.* Washington, DC: CIA, 1985.

White, William. *Subminiature Photography.* Stoneham, MA: Butterworth, 1990.

Wright, Peter. *The Spycatcher's Encyclopedia of Espionage.* Port Melbourne, Australia: Heinemann, 1991.

Locks, Picks, and Clicks. (No publisher or date.)

Index